To:

From:

Date:

30 Days to RUNNING GREAT STORES

30 Days to RUNNING GREAT STORES

Strategies to Build Unstoppable Teams, Boost Sales, and Transform Your Store

Rachel A. Williamson

FIRST EDITION

30 DAYS TO RUNNING GREAT STORES
Strategies to Build Unstoppable Teams, Boost Sales, and Transform Your Store

ISBN 978-1-5445-5099-2 *Hardcover*
978-1-5445-5098-5 *Paperback*
978-1-5445-5100-5 *Ebook*

First and foremost, to God be the glory.

To my husband, Vic—
thank you for your unwavering love and support
through all the nights, weekends, and miles on the road.
Your constant belief in me made this possible.

To my daughter, Alexandra—
thank you for championing my retail journey,
for always bringing the voice of Gen Z to the table,
and for believing I could write this book.
Your encouragement kept me moving forward.

And to Store Leaders everywhere, whether we've met or not—
your passion, resilience, and dedication to this craft
have inspired me more than you'll ever know.
You've filled my bucket time and time again.
This book is for you.

Contents

Introduction

Hey, You, the One Who Lives and Breathes Retail.

If there's one thing I know, it's that you want the secret to being number one. Not because you crave the spotlight, but because you *love* retail—it's in your blood. You live for the energy, the challenge, and the win. And in retail, success is measured in results. Every day comes with a report card…yesterday's numbers. And here's the truth: We're only as good as those results.

This isn't your average leadership book. It's filled with proven behaviors—the same ones that fueled my success in retail—and they'll work for you too, when you apply them.

My career started early. I was fourteen, still in high school, and scooping ice cream at Baskin-Robbins. Every shift, I'd hop onto the counter to slide flavor signs off the wall and say, "Sorry, we're out." I watched sales walk out the door because our cake freezer was often empty. Customers didn't always want to place an order and come back—they wanted it *now*.

So, I approached the owner with my observations and recommendations. He challenged me: "If you can do better, go for it." And I did. Age didn't matter. What mattered was understanding what truly drove revenue: happy customers, all thirty-one flavors in stock, and a freezer full of cakes, pies, and clown cones ready to go.

At fourteen, my insights didn't come from a college degree or an MBA. They came from watching disappointed customers—and being determined to fix it. After that conversation, we never ran out of flavors again. The cake freezer was full. Sales exploded. That was the start of my obsession with ***running great stores***.

From there, I moved into apparel and beauty retail—working with small independent retailers and eventually leading flagship locations for national brands. I steadily moved up, from store manager to area manager, then to district manager, regional learning manager, and eventually vice president of store operations, overseeing one thousand stores across North America. At every level, I led top-performing teams and broke sales records.

The truth is, I made plenty of mistakes along the way. Gratefully, I had mentors and leaders who guided me, challenged me, and believed in me. I also couldn't get enough leadership books—they shaped how I think, lead, and show up for others. In these pages, I'll share some of my favorites so you can read them too.

My approach to running great stores never changed. Listen. Observe. Solve. Every store performed. Owners loved me. Customers came back. Revenue soared. I was promoted quickly, again and again.

I'm not telling you this to brag—I'm telling you because the strategies in this book are proven.

Every one of the more than one million brick-and-mortar retail stores in America has the potential to be great. And the three hundred thousand in Canada. And the millions more around the world. But potential doesn't drive results...leadership and execution do.

These thirty principles aren't a menu to pick and choose from—they're designed to work together. *The magic happens in consistent application, not selective adoption.*

Retail has been my passion for as long as I can remember, and I've written this book to share what I know works.

Here's the thing: Retail is often seen as a temporary job, a stepping stone until something "better" comes along. But it doesn't have to be that way. *Retail can be an incredible, fulfilling career path*—it certainly has been for me.

So why do people quit retail? Because they're not successful. They're not getting trained. They're not getting raises. They're not getting promoted. It's time to stop putting your career in the hands of your immediate boss—and start *owning your success.*

Whether you have a college degree or not, whether you're new to retail or a tenured retail leader, this book will help you hit the ground running—or gain momentum as a standout, top-performing leader.

I've led both boutique brands and major national retailers, and no matter the banner, I consistently ranked among the top-performing store and district managers. That success wasn't about luck—it came from focus, consistency, and a repeatable approach to leading people, serving customers, and running high-performing stores.

I've also witnessed firsthand how external disruptions—from economic shifts to global events like COVID-19—can challenge even the most established retailers. While these events are often blamed for store closures, the truth is that many struggling stores were poorly run to begin with.

My goal is to ensure your brand isn't one of them. Don't let your store disappear. Equip every leader with this book—and watch your results soar.

Here's the good news: *It's not a secret formula.* There are specific, teachable habits that drive retail excellence—and this book delivers them.

Inside, you'll find thirty daily principles designed to sharpen your leadership, build a high-performing team, and elevate your store's sales results. These aren't theories—they're real-world strategies that deliver measurable results.

It will be best to start on Day 1 and move sequentially through Day 30; however this is your playbook. Use it daily if you can. But don't let perfection get in the way of progress. Start where you are, apply the concepts, and watch what happens.

You'll also see a few "Rachel-isms" sprinkled throughout—sayings I've used throughout my career that teammates began repeating back to me over the years. In fact, more than one person has joked, "You should write a book of Rachel-isms someday!" While this isn't that book, you'll definitely find them woven into the pages—simple phrases that stick, because they work.

Retail doesn't get better by accident. It gets better when leaders like you show up with purpose. One of the best ways to practice is to follow the "Time to Take Action" recommendation each day. Real plays are actual people in their own roles, dealing with a challenge they are facing. They are more authentic than "role-plays" with the goal to solve the real issue rather than fake acting.

My recommendation…at the end of each day, ask yourself: "What did I do today that moved my store forward?" Write it down. Keep a small notebook or digital log. Reflection builds awareness, reinforces positive habits, and identifies gaps for tomorrow.

I'm cheering you on—and committed to helping you succeed.

Let's get started.

What's Inside This Book

WEEK 1

Lead Yourself First

Day 1: Own Your Leadership

Day 2: Model the Behavior You Expect

Day 3: Set Clear Expectations

Day 4: Build Trust Through Communication

Day 5: Develop a Positive and Solution-Oriented Mindset

Day 6: Adapt and Stay Resilient

Day 7: EQ Is Your Superpower

Recap: Power in the Pause

REAL WINS, REAL LESSONS

As the store manager of a small, independently owned retail shop, my team and I were dedicated to providing every customer with a great experience. One afternoon, a man came in searching for a birthday gift for his wife. Together, we found something special, wrapped it with care, and he left smiling.

The next day, he called.

Turns out, he was the district manager for the Gap, and he wanted to recruit me. He said something that stuck: "It's time to move from small brands to a place where you can really grow your career." The catch? I'd have to start over—as an assistant manager, no less! The Gap store was doing five times the volume of the store I had been managing, and he needed to see how I handled the transition.

Sounds fair, right?

It took a moment to swallow my pride. But he added, "If you're as good as I think you are, you won't be in that role for long." He was right. Within thirty days, I was promoted to store manager.

When that promotion came, it was in the same store where I had been working as an assistant manager. To put it mildly, this store had its challenges: high turnover, low morale, hideous shrink issues, and a sales team that had lost its spark. More than one person warned, *You're taking on a mess.*

But walking in, what I carried with me wasn't experience managing big teams or big volume—it was mindset. A belief that effort, consistency, and genuine care could change the culture.

I didn't wait to be told what to do—I rolled up my sleeves and got to work. I started by sitting down with every team member, one by one, just to hear their story. I wanted them to feel seen, heard, and part of something bigger. Then I introduced a few small rituals that changed everything: a quick huddle to kick off the day, end-of-shift shout-outs to recognize wins, and weekly goal reviews to keep us focused. I kept the energy positive, the expectations clear, and my door wide open.

We chased volume with intention and made conversion our North Star. But more than that, we created a place where customers felt something different—something better. Before long, they weren't just coming back to shop. They were asking for job applications. They wanted to be part of the team they loved buying from.

Slowly, things shifted. Team members started showing up early, reengaging with customers, and bringing ideas to the table. Within weeks, we were hitting our numbers. Within ninety days, we were leading the district. Seasoned store managers were calling me, asking what I was doing so they could do it too. We openly shared as we wanted the entire district to soar.

This wasn't a team of retail rock stars—at least, not at first. But *belief is contagious*. And when people know they're seen and supported, they start showing up differently.

LESSON LEARNED

Leadership isn't about having the most experience. It's about the energy you bring, the consistency you model, and the way you choose to show up—every...single...day.

RACHEL-*ism*

One of my more famous "Rachel-isms" is:

"What I Believe Drives How I Behave, and How I Behave Drives My Results."

While I didn't create this saying (not sure who is the original author), it has been adapted to how I lead and get results.

This phrase isn't just true for me and for you...it's true for every person on your team. Beliefs are powerful. They're the invisible drivers behind every action, every habit, and every outcome. If you want different results, you can't just bark new instructions. You have to understand what someone believes to be true and then influence that.

I was the district manager with eighteen locations in my district. There was one very high-volume, low-square-footage store that struggled to keep the back room organized. To complicate matters, they also had an off-site storage facility on the upper floor of the mall. Every visit, I'd end up staying late, helping to clean it up and organize what was in the back room versus what was at off-site upstairs.

At first, I loved helping, teaching the team how to think about their back room. But with every visit, there was no improvement. I thought this was a performance issue. Over time, I became exhausted being the DM who also doubled as the back room fixer. My regional finally asked me, "Do you know *why* she doesn't keep it organized?"

So, I asked the store manager that very question.

What I discovered changed everything. She didn't think back rooms mattered. In her words, "The customer never sees it, so I focus all my energy on the sales floor."

That belief was the problem—not her work ethic. But here is the truth: the messy back room *was* impacting the customer. The floor couldn't stay full during peak times because no one could find what they needed in the chaos of the back room. It wasn't a visual issue. It was a *productivity* issue. I told her something one of my favorite bosses to date, Jeanne St. Pierre, had once told me: "The back room is the engine of the car. If it's not humming, your sales floor won't run right either."

Once she understood that—and believed it to be true—her behavior changed. So did her results. I never had to clean up that back room again because her team kept it humming from that day forward. It also impacted her sales floor and their ability to keep it full during peaks. The result? She zoomed to one of the top ten volume stores in a chain of over 1,600 locations.

As a leader, your job isn't to command tasks. It's to uncover beliefs. Because when beliefs shift, behaviors follow—and that's how real, lasting change happens.

DAY 1

Own Your Leadership

TITLES DON'T INSPIRE TEAMS. PEOPLE DO.

True leadership isn't granted by a job description. It's earned every single shift through how you show up, how you treat your people, and the standards you hold. You're not just managing a store; you're creating the energy that drives it. Think of yourself as the thermostat, not the thermometer.

Your vibe becomes the culture. Your standards set the pace. Your follow-through either builds trust or breaks it.

Lesson from the Field

When I was promoted to the new twelve-thousand-square-foot superstore as the general manager at the Gap, I thought the title would speak for itself. But within a week, I realized my team wasn't impressed with my title—they were watching my behavior. The moment I started showing up early, staying late, and owning every detail, everything shifted…and so did they.

When you walk in with intention, your team notices. When you lead with clarity, they respond. When you care—really care—they give you their best. Leadership is a daily decision. Make it yours.

What Great Leaders Do

Lead with Purpose, Not Just a To-Do List

- ✓ Show up with intention and energy.
- ✓ Consider how each choice impacts the customer and team.
- ✓ Align every action to the store's bigger goals.

Own the Store like It's Yours

- ✓ Walk the store with a critical eye, not just a clipboard.
- ✓ Treat every detail—from windows to restrooms—as a reflection of your leadership.
- ✓ Make decisions that elevate the customer experience and business results.

Build Trust Through Consistency

- ✓ Follow through on what you say, every time.
- ✓ Lean into difficult conversations with clarity and respect.
- ✓ Set the tone by modeling integrity and accountability.

Make One Confident Decision Daily

- ✓ A great leader doesn't second-guess every move.
- ✓ Trust your knowledge, your gut, and your experience. Whether it's adjusting coverage for a sudden traffic spike or rearranging a feature table for better product flow, make one decision each day that impacts your store's performance.

Coach in the Moment

- ✓ The best training doesn't happen behind a closed door—it happens on the floor.
- ✓ See something done right? Praise it on the spot. Notice a misstep? Correct it kindly, immediately, and with context. This keeps standards high and shows your team that every moment is an opportunity to improve.

FINAL THOUGHT

You don't need permission to lead—you just need purpose. The best store managers show up each day determined to make a difference. Start there. Everything else builds from that commitment.

TIME TO TAKE ACTION

- ☐ Pick one leadership move you've been avoiding. Maybe it's addressing a behavior you've let slide. Maybe it's praising a team member who's overdue for recognition. Maybe it's resetting a store standard or walking the floor at peak traffic. Whatever it is, stop waiting. Your store improves the moment you lead with courage.

DAY 2

Model the Behavior You Expect

WANT A ROCK-STAR TEAM? BE THE ROCK STAR, FIRST.

If you're dreaming of a team that owns their work, keeps it cool under pressure, and shows up ready to win, you've got to lead the way.

Your energy *is* the atmosphere. Your standards *are* the bar. If you start cutting corners, guess what? They'll grab the scissors too. But if you're showing up prepared, focused, and fired up? Your team will follow suit.

Lesson from the Field

I'll never forget the time we were slammed on a Saturday at the Gap, and the fitting rooms were a mess. I didn't call someone over; I grabbed a rack and started rehanging. Without saying a word, the rest of the team jumped in. That moment reminded me: When the leader sets the pace, the team follows. From that day forward, the team used to say, "Let's get to it before she does!" I loved it.

What separates good retail leaders from great ones? It's not just what you know or how hard you work; it's your attitude. Always. The strongest leaders are built on mindset, character, and how you *show up*—especially when no one's watching. Leadership is seriously contagious. Make yours worth catching.

What Great Leaders Do

Model the Standard

You want your team to deliver an exceptional experience? Show them what that looks like.

- ✓ Make it a point to greet customers warmly, ask open-ended questions, and sincerely thank them.
- ✓ Handle a difficult return with grace.
- ✓ Pitch in when the fitting room is overflowing or a line forms at checkout.
- ✓ Invite your team to observe you for a few minutes—then flip it: Observe *them* and offer real-time coaching. Don't wait for the perfect teaching moment—*create it.*

Build a Culture of Respect

If you're working to shift negativity, gossip, or low morale, listen to how you speak—both to your team and about your team.

- ✓ Do you celebrate wins publicly?
- ✓ Do you offer feedback privately and respectfully?
- ✓ Do you gossip about your team to others?
- ✓ Do you show appreciation—even on tough days? Your tone becomes *their tone—what you model gets mirrored.*

Show Up Ready

If you are trying to get your team to arrive on time, ask yourself:

- ✓ Am I consistently early and ready before my shift starts?
- ✓ Do I greet them when they arrive with energy and consistency?
- ✓ Do I begin team huddles promptly at the scheduled time—even if only two people are present?

Start by modeling punctuality every day. Create a culture where being on time means being prepared, not just walking through the door.

Start Clean, Stay Clean

Want your store to look sharp all day, not just for visits? Pick up trash, straighten products, fix signage, and wipe down surfaces as you walk through. When your team sees you do it, without complaint, they realize it's part of everyone's role. Over time, they will follow suit. It's contagious.

FINAL THOUGHT

Your actions set the tone. Your team is always watching—not because they are trying to catch you slipping, but because they are learning what is acceptable, expected, and rewarded.

TIME TO TAKE ACTION

- ☐ Pick one behavior you want to see more of in your store—and lead it by example today. Show, don't tell.
- ☐ Then, take ten minutes at the end of your shift to reflect: Did anyone follow your lead?

DAY 3

Set Clear Expectations

CONFUSED TEAMS CAN'T CRUSH GOALS

When expectations are fuzzy, everything gets wobbly—results, morale, and your customers' trust. One great experience, one not-so-great one? That's a recipe for "Thanks, but we're shopping elsewhere."

Lesson from the Field

When I was new to the director of store operations role for Limited Too, I noticed performance gaps almost always traced back to unclear expectations. We struggled with inconsistent execution across the 580 stores. In partnership with the district and regional managers, we got to the root cause and launched a retail playbook that clearly outlined expectations—from opening checklists to customer greetings. Within weeks, store performance metrics improved, and frontline teams felt more confident because they knew exactly what was expected. Clear expectations turned confusion into consistency and boosted results across the chain. Clarity became our competitive edge.

Here's the deal: Your team *wants* to do well. But if they don't know what "great" looks like, how can they deliver? Clarity isn't control—it's kindness. It's a game plan, a cheat code, a "You bet, I know what I'm doing today!" Your team cannot meet expectations that they don't know exist!

Great leaders don't wing it. They draw the map, drop a pin, and make sure their team knows exactly how to win.

What Great Leaders Do

When your team knows what great looks like, they can deliver it confidently. When they don't, they guess—and *that's where standards slip*. When your store standards slip, customers notice.

Think of expectations as the playbook your team *wants*. It's not micromanaging—it's *clarity*, and clarity builds trust, speed, and confidence.

Whether it's how you greet a customer, keep the store looking amazing, or own a task from start to finish—it's your job to set the standard, communicate it clearly, and reinforce it with consistency.

Communicate Expectations Clearly and Consistently

- ✓ Share specific, measurable goals that everyone understands and can act on.
- ✓ Use simple, direct language—no jargon or vague instructions.
- ✓ Repeat and reinforce expectations regularly through team huddles, meetings, and one-on-ones.

Model the Standards You Set

- ✓ Demonstrate the behaviors and quality you expect from your team every day.
- ✓ Hold yourself accountable to the same expectations without exception.
- ✓ Give real-time feedback to guide and support improvement.

Empower Your Team to Own Their Roles

- ✓ Invite questions and encourage your team to seek clarity when unsure.
- ✓ Recognize and celebrate when expectations are met or exceeded.
- ✓ Provide tools and resources that make it easy for team members to succeed.

FINAL THOUGHT

Accountability without clarity is just frustration. Accountability with clarity is unstoppable.

TIME TO TAKE ACTION

- ☐ Pick one process or standard in your store and define it so clearly that no one could misunderstand it.
- ☐ Share it with your team and follow up within a week to check progress.

DAY 4

Build Trust Through Communication

TRUST ISN'T BUILT THROUGH SILENCE—IT'S BUILT THROUGH COMMUNICATION

The more your team hears from you, the more they'll trust you. Be honest, transparent, and approachable so your team members feel safe bringing you both problems and ideas.

Lesson from the Field

I once spent three straight days behind a closed office door, heads down on a massive assignment. Unintentionally, my silence had the team on edge. They thought something was wrong. A quick huddle to explain what I was working on instantly eased their worry, and I learned that even when you're busy, communication is leadership.

Silence creates assumptions. When there is silence, your team will tell themselves a story, and it's usually not a good one. So why are we silent? Too often, busyness and stress cause us to focus on what is urgent instead of what matters most. We focus on our to-do list instead of people, and our own survival instead of building thriving relationships. We must slow down to communicate.

Communication creates connection. When your team knows you're in their corner—and that you'll listen without judgment—they'll bring their best to the table.

What Great Leaders Do

Great leaders create a culture of transparency and openness—even when the conversations are tough. They don't just hand out directives; they explain the *why* behind decisions, so their team understands the broader vision and their part in it. They communicate both wins and challenges with honesty and balance. Avoid sugarcoating the good or dwelling too long on the bad. This approach builds trust, invites collaboration, and helps everyone feel informed, included, and aligned.

Actively Listen and Value Input with Empathy

- ✓ Create safe spaces for feedback. Hold regular huddles where team members can share ideas, concerns, or observations without fear of judgment.
- ✓ Respond to concerns, even if you can't solve them immediately.
- ✓ Implement their ideas when possible.
- ✓ When an employee is going through a personal challenge, acknowledge it. This builds immense loyalty and trust.
- ✓ Deliver feedback constructively. Using the Situation-Behavior-Impact (SBI) model focuses on the action, not the person, and offers support. This model is a simple feedback method that helps you describe the situation, explain the observed behavior, and share the impact it had, making feedback more specific, objective, and actionable.

Demonstrate Consistency and Reliability

- ✓ Follow through on promises. If you say you'll provide specific training, schedule it and follow through.
- ✓ Ensure that what you tell one employee isn't contradicted by what you tell another, or what corporate communicates. If there are slight variations, explain why.
- ✓ Team members should know what to expect from you in terms of your communication style, reactions, and decision-making. This builds psychological safety.
- ✓ Avoid "mood swings" or inconsistent reactions to similar situations. If a certain mistake is acceptable one day but results in severe reprimand the next, trust breaks down.

Show Authenticity and Empathy

- ✓ Be approachable. Your body language, tone, and willingness to engage in informal conversation make a big difference.
- ✓ Admit mistakes. This humanizes you and shows you're accountable.

Give Clarity and Conciseness

- ✓ Give clear instructions. When delegating a task, ensure the employee understands *what* needs to be done, *by when*, and *what success looks like*. Avoid jargon or acronyms.
- ✓ Confirm understanding. After giving instructions, ask open-ended questions.

FINAL THOUGHT

By consistently demonstrating effective communication practices, a retail store leader doesn't just manage a team; they build a highly engaged, resilient, and trusting workforce that is more likely to go the extra mile for the store, the customers, and each other.

Notes

TIME TO TAKE ACTION

- ☐ Identify a task you frequently assign but often doesn't get completed to your standards.
- ☐ Rework how you describe the expectation for the task and see what the outcome is.
- ☐ Now, leverage this learning every time you assign tasks to a member of the team.

DAY 5

Develop a Positive and Solution-Oriented Mindset

RETAIL IS UNPREDICTABLE—BUT YOUR MINDSET IS YOUR ANCHOR

Problems will come. It's part of the job. But great leaders don't get stuck in the problem—they get to work on the solution.

When you model a positive, forward-focused attitude, your team learns to stay calm under pressure and find a way forward.

Lesson from the Field

When I was an area manager for Ann Taylor, we had a major floor set to complete in advance of the head of stores coming to visit. Half our shipment was delayed, and tensions were rising fast. Instead of joining the stress spiral, I gathered the team, acknowledged the setback, and we quickly shifted focus to what could be done. That mindset kept morale high—and we still opened the doors the next day with a store we were proud of. We had a great visit, not because everything had gone as planned, but because the team had approached the challenge with positivity.

Positivity isn't about ignoring challenges—it's about choosing to lead through them.

What Great Leaders Do

Great leaders stay grounded and calm, especially when pressure is high. Instead of reacting impulsively, they take a moment to respond with intention—anchoring themselves and their team in the facts. By staying steady and focused, they help others see a clear path forward, even in tough moments. They're mindful of their tone, body language, and energy, knowing that their presence sets the emotional tone for the team.

Lead with a Forward-Focused, Solution-Driven Mindset

- ✓ Ask, "What's the next right step?" instead of getting stuck in what went wrong.
- ✓ Encourage creative thinking and empower your team to bring solutions.
- ✓ Reinforce the belief that challenges are temporary, but *how we respond defines us.*

Pivot from What Went Wrong? to What Can We Do?

- ✓ Don't dwell, debrief. Quickly assess what happened, extract the learning, and move forward.
- ✓ Shift the team's focus from blame to ownership: "What's in our control right now?"
- ✓ Turn every challenge into a leadership moment by guiding the team toward the solution, not just the problem.

FINAL THOUGHT

By consistently applying these practices, a retail store leader transforms their store from a place that reacts to crises into one that proactively innovates, adapts, and thrives amid the inherent unpredictability of the retail world.

TIME TO TAKE ACTION

- ☐ Reflect on a past challenge. How did you handle it? What will you do differently next time?
- ☐ Although it can be stressful, ask your boss for their point of view. When you are open to hearing how others perceive you, you are on the track to true growth.

DAY 6

Foster Accountability

ACCOUNTABILITY ISN'T CONTROL—IT'S COMMITMENT

High-impact leaders create a culture where expectations are clear and follow-through is the norm. When everyone owns their role, trust is built, and performance rises.

Accountability isn't about catching people doing something wrong; it's about building a team that takes pride in ***doing things right***. Leaders don't assume tasks get done. They actively check in and provide timely feedback. This consistent follow-up creates a rhythm where accountability is part of everyday work.

The Difference Between Accountability and Responsibility?

- ✓ *Responsibility* is the task; you're assigned something to do.
- ✓ *Accountability* is the ownership; you make sure it actually gets done and done well.

Lesson from the Field

I once worked with a store that couldn't figure out why closing tasks were always incomplete. The store manager insisted she had "told the team a hundred times." But when we walked the floor at closing, it was clear—the team wasn't aligned. No checklist. No walk-through. No follow-up. We implemented a simple end-of-day checklist and added a five-minute huddle to assign ownership. Within a week, closing execution improved dramatically. The team now knew exactly what was expected—and someone was checking. Accountability starts with clarity.

Strong teams aren't just responsible—they're accountable. And that mindset starts with you.

What Great Leaders Do

Every team member should understand their daily tasks, priorities, and the standards expected of them. One of my favorite ways to build accountability at every level in a store is by assigning clear areas of responsibility to each manager. This concept, once commonly known as DORs (divisions of responsibility), has fallen out of use in many retailers, and standards are slipping because of it.

But what's old is new again. DORs create ownership by assigning leaders to key areas like people, customer experience, and operations (which often includes visual merchandising). Each leader is responsible not only for execution but also for:

- ✓ Training the team
- ✓ Maintaining high standards
- ✓ Delivering a consistent, high-impact experience for every customer through their DOR

Trust, but Verify

Trust but verify is a powerful leadership mindset. It allows you to show confidence in your team while still holding them accountable. Even the most dependable team members benefit from clear expectations and regular follow-up. Trust that the work is being done, but don't stop there. Circle back. Check in. Walk the floor. Review the results. Verifying doesn't mean you doubt them; it means you care enough to make sure the standards are being met every time.

Model Accountability in Your Actions

Accountability isn't just top-down; it's personal. Strong leaders own their mistakes, meet their commitments, and model what follow-through looks like. When leaders show this kind of vulnerability and discipline, it sets the tone for the entire team.

Give Positive Reinforcement and Coaching

- ✓ Celebrate when commitments are met. Recognition reinforces great behavior and boosts morale.
- ✓ When standards aren't met, coach with curiosity and clarity. Ask questions, offer support, and guide your team toward solutions—without blame.

Leverage Peer Accountability

Over time, high-functioning teams begin to hold each other accountable. This shared ownership builds trust, strengthens team culture, and reduces the need for constant managerial intervention—without lowering expectations.

FINAL THOUGHT

Accountability is a muscle. It grows stronger with daily reps and the right leadership mindset.

When you create clear expectations, follow through consistently, and build a culture of shared ownership, your team won't just meet goals—they'll exceed them with pride and confidence.

Accountability isn't a "once and done" activity. It's the heartbeat of a high-performing store.

Notes

TIME TO TAKE ACTION

- ☐ Today, ask each team member to name one specific goal they will accomplish before the end of their shift.
- ☐ Then circle back before they leave—recognize the win or coach the gap. That's what real-time accountability looks like.

DAY 7

EQ Is Your Superpower

WHY BEING PEOPLE-SMART WINS WHERE METRICS ALONE FALL SHORT

Emotional intelligence, often called EQ, is your ability to recognize and regulate your own emotions while also tuning into the emotions of others. It's what makes someone "people smart."

Leaders with high EQ know how to read a room, respond rather than react, and create trust in the moment.

In a retail setting, EQ is a superpower. It helps you navigate difficult conversations, defuse tension, boost morale, and support your team through both the highs and the lows of daily store life. You can have stellar results. Crush every metric. Be the top performer.

And yet, you can still get passed over for promotion. Why? EQ might be the missing piece.

Lesson from the Field

When I was a district manager, one of my best stores suddenly tanked in sales. The data told me what was happening, but the second I walked in, I could feel why. The team was tense, the smiles forced. I pulled the manager aside and simply asked, "Are you okay?" She broke down. A personal crisis had overwhelmed her, and the team was absorbing her stress. We put a plan in place, gave her support, and within weeks, sales rebounded—not because of new promotions, but because the store's energy had shifted. Numbers tell the story. EQ changes the ending.

EQ isn't just a "nice-to-have"—it's essential for stepping into roles with more responsibility, especially in multiunit leadership. Leading through others, navigating tough conversations, staying calm under pressure—it all comes back to EQ. If the promotions aren't coming, even with strong performance, it's worth asking your boss for their perspective. Is EQ holding you back?

What Great Leaders Do

As a retail store leader, your ability to understand and manage your own emotions, as well as to perceive and influence the emotions of others, is arguably as critical as your business acumen. It's the capacity to navigate the human element of your business, from motivating your team and de-escalating customer conflicts to adapting to unexpected challenges. A high-EQ leader fosters a more empathetic, productive, and resilient store culture, ultimately driving better results.

Understand Your Own Impact

Feeling impatient during a busy rush? Take a deep breath, step away for thirty seconds if possible, and remind yourself to remain calm and supportive for your team, rather than adding to the stress.

Manage Your Reactions

Instead of reacting defensively or mirroring their anger, remain calm, lower your voice, and use empathetic language ("I understand your frustration"). Steady demeanor helps de-escalate the customer and models professional behavior for your team.

Understand Other Perspectives

Don't jump to conclusions about performance; pull the employee aside privately. Listen nonjudgmentally and offer support rather than criticism.

Inspire Your Team

During a challenging sales period, understand that simply demanding more effort won't work. Tap into what genuinely motivates your team (e.g., competition, recognition, skill development). Frame targets not just as numbers but as opportunities for personal growth or team achievement, celebrating small wins along the way.

Build Strong Relationships

- ✓ Actively foster a positive team environment by mediating minor conflicts effectively, encouraging collaboration, and facilitating open communication. You're known for being approachable and fair, making your team feel safe to voice concerns and contribute ideas.
- ✓ Build rapport with regular customers by remembering their names, preferences, or even details about their lives (if shared). This makes them feel valued beyond just their purchases.

FINAL THOUGHT

By consciously practicing these elements of EQ, you don't just manage a store; you lead a thriving team and cultivate a loyal customer base, transforming challenges into opportunities for growth and deeper connection.

Notes

TIME TO TAKE ACTION

- ☐ Do a quick *emotional check-in* today with yourself and at least two team members. Go beyond the surface-level "How are you?" Look for tone, body language, and energy shifts. Listen actively. And if something feels off, gently ask questions like "Is everything okay? You seem upset."
- ☐ Offer support or adjust how you interact. EQ is about *meeting people where they are*—and leading them forward with empathy.

Power in the Pause

WEEK 1 RECAP: LEADING FROM THE INSIDE OUT

This week focused on building a strong leadership foundation. Before you can lead others, you have to lead yourself with clarity, consistency, and confidence. Take a moment to revisit the key habits you've worked on:

Focus Areas

Day 1—Own Your Leadership

Leadership isn't about a title—it's about daily actions and the standard you set.

Day 2—Model the Behavior You Expect

Your team mirrors your actions. If you want energy, and ownership, you have to go first.

Day 3—Set Clear Expectations

Clarity drives consistency. Don't assume they know. Be specific, be direct, and follow through.

Day 4—Build Trust Through Communication

Trust grows when leaders are present, honest, and approachable. Keep the door open.

Day 5—Develop a Positive and Solution-Oriented Mindset

Don't dwell on the problem—model possibility. Positivity drives performance.

Day 6—Foster Accountability

Accountability isn't just assigning tasks—it's ensuring follow-through. Every team member should know exactly what's expected, the standards they must meet, and that you *will* check in. Consistent follow-up reinforces that what matters gets measured, and what gets measured gets done.

Day 7—Demonstrate Emotional Intelligence (EQ)

Awareness of your emotions—and others'—helps you lead with empathy, not ego.

REFLECT AND RESET

What habit made the biggest impact this week?

Where did you notice a shift in your leadership or team dynamic?

What do you want to carry forward into next week?

RACHEL-*ism*

Strong stores start with strong leaders—and strong leadership starts with self-awareness.

WEEK 2

Elevate the Customer Experience

REAL WINS, REAL LESSONS

It was a rainy Tuesday afternoon, the kind that was usually slow in our shop, tucked inside the Continent, an outdoor shopping center in Columbus, Ohio. The door opened, and in walked a mom and her daughter. They had shopped with us before, but this visit felt different.

One of my team members recognized them and greeted them back with warmth and zero pressure, instantly making them feel at ease. Her mom explained they were looking for a birthday dress. Then, in a low voice, she added, "She hasn't wanted to shop in months." It had been a hard year filled with bullying, self-doubt, and the health struggles that accompany it. Her daughter's confidence had been shaken. She was soon turning eighteen and looked unsure of herself.

I joined shortly after and began a quiet conversation with the mom and the young woman—asking what she was envisioning for herself, the colors she liked, and the styles she absolutely didn't like. Together, we picked out three dresses and showed her to the fitting room. Just a few choices. No push. No rush.

When she stepped out in the third dress—a simple navy wrap—something changed. Her posture straightened. Her eyes lit up. She smiled, really smiled.

"You don't just look beautiful," we told her. "You look like *yourself.*"

Her mom's eyes welled with tears. They bought the dress, a pair of shoes, and simple jewelry. Before they left, I walked over and said, "We loved having you here today. You truly made our day."

Three days later, a handwritten card arrived.

"You didn't just sell us a dress," the mom wrote. "You helped my daughter see herself again. Thank you for your kindness and care."

If you're wondering what happened next, she came back that summer, this time as part of our team. She worked with us during her college breaks, helping others feel seen, just like she had. Because inside the four walls of that store, she felt safe. Accepted. Appreciated. Loved.

The Customer Impact

Great retail leadership isn't just about selling products—it's about training teams to ***listen deeply, personalize the experience***, and ***see the customer***. When that happens, confidence can be restored. Joy can be sparked. And lives can be changed.

That kind of magic starts at the top with leaders who build a culture where people matter more than transactions.

DAY 8

Make Exceptional Customer Service Nonnegotiable

EXCEPTIONAL SERVICE SHOULDN'T BE A GOAL—IT SHOULD BE THE STANDARD

Customers don't come back because of your products alone; they come back because of how they feel when they shop with you.

As the leader, it's your job to define what exceptional customer service looks like, model it daily, and hold your team to that level consistently. Set the bar high and make it nonnegotiable—because average service won't keep customers coming back.

Lesson from the Field

I was conducting a field visit with a district manager, and the store manager was talking to us about their business. Mid-sentence, they paused, excused themselves from our conversation, and walked over to assist a customer with an item out of reach. That customer was grateful, left with a smile, and the next day came back with a friend. Great service doesn't just sell products; it creates advocates. I loved that the store leader understood that the customer came first and served her without apology to us.

Mark Ryski, author of *Store Traffic Is a Gift*, once told me, "Customers should be treated like the nonrenewable resource that they are." That is the lens that I look through when I spend time in stores. Can you visualize what that looks like in your store?

What Great Leaders Do

Define and Model Service Excellence Every Day

- ✓ Ensure you've clearly outlined what a great customer experience looks, sounds, and feels like in your store.
- ✓ Coach in real time when standards are met and when they aren't. Expectations should be nonnegotiable.

Create a Culture Where Service Comes First

- ✓ Prioritize people over tasks, always choosing the customer in front of you over the task at hand.
- ✓ Recognize and celebrate team members who deliver outstanding service moments.

- ✓ Empower team members to make things right without needing permission or escalation.

You Build Confidence Through Practice and Feedback

- ✓ Use real play (more fun than role-play) regularly to strengthen skills and build comfort handling tough interactions.
- ✓ Create a safe space for learning, where feedback and service improvement are part of your culture—not a punishment.

FINAL THOUGHT

When a store leader clearly defines expectations, models the behaviors, and holds the team accountable, service standards become more than just rules—they become culture. And when "great service" becomes your baseline, *exceptional service* becomes your reputation.

TIME TO TAKE ACTION

- ☐ Observe the customer experiences in your store. Rotate, having your team members observe with you, and ask them what they see. This is how you know what they believe to be true about what superior customer service looks like.

DAY 9

KPIs and Behaviors That Drive Results

DON'T JUST WATCH THE NUMBERS—COACH THE BEHAVIOR THAT CREATES THEM

KPIs or key performance indicators aren't just reports to glance at. They're a roadmap to your store's performance. But here's the truth: *Metrics measure what's already happened.* If you want to change the *outcome*, you have to focus on the *behaviors* behind the numbers.

Traffic and conversion are your most powerful tools to leverage to understand the opportunities that exist to grow the business. They tell you not just what's happening—but *why*. Low conversion? It's not a number problem—it's a people and process problem. Are we greeting customers with intention? Are we helping them find what they need? Are we giving them reasons to buy?

Lesson from the Field

When I was a district manager, one of my stores had soft conversion for weeks. The store manager kept reviewing the numbers but never left the back office. During a visit, we observed the floor together. It was obvious that customers were being greeted with "Let me know if you need anything" and then left alone. A quick coaching moment turned into a new greeting approach, and conversion started climbing within days. She also realized that being heads down in the back room was causing her to miss what was actually happening on the floor.

Data is a starting point to ask questions, but nothing replaces observing in the moment to see what the customer sees. Strong leaders don't just report KPIs. They diagnose, coach, and course-correct in real time. Because great results don't come from spreadsheets. They come from observing, coaching, and leading right from the sales floor.

What Great Leaders Do

Real-time performance monitoring and coaching means keeping your finger on the pulse of the store's performance throughout the day.

Set Sales Goals

Every day should start with a clear sales goal—whether your company provides one or not. Connect it to your monthly target, a comp over last year's same-day results, or another key metric that matters. Setting a daily goal sharpens focus and drives performance. I love the saying, "What gets measured gets done," because I've seen it prove true throughout my career. When you focus on the number and share it with the team, it becomes a shared priority.

Chase Results

- ✓ Hourly reads at the POS reinforce what is happening. I have often seen a store miss the day by a small amount. Why? Sometimes it is because the team was not taking reads and didn't realize they were that close to making their day. Other teams worked hard and minimized the miss it could have been!
- ✓ Once you see the actual results, connect the metrics to behaviors.
    - ▷ If sales are tracking below goal, consider whether you're seeing fewer customers or if customers are buying less.
    - ▷ If ATV (average transaction value) is low, focus on upselling and cross-selling techniques.
    - ▷ If UPT (units per transaction) is low, it may indicate a need for better product recommendations instead of single-item sales.
    - ▷ If conversion is down, prioritize engaging every customer. Watch to see if the team is dropping tasks to assist customers.
    - ▷ This isn't data for data's sake—it's a prompt for immediate coaching. Great leaders constantly link what they see on the screen to the behaviors happening on the sales floor.
    - ▷ Keep track of where you are in the week, the month, and the year. This is where you will maximize your store's revenue!

FINAL THOUGHT

By integrating these practices into your daily routine, you're not just managing a store; you're cultivating a sales-driven culture where every interaction is an opportunity to serve the customer better and drive revenue.

TIME TO TAKE ACTION

- [ ] Identify one critical sales metric where a focused increase, driven by the right employee behaviors, would significantly elevate your sales performance.

DAY 10

Maximize Traffic

STOP LOSING SALES TO INVISIBLE SERVICE

The truth is, most lost sales don't happen because of bad service—they happen because of *no* service. Customers walk in, browse for a few minutes, and leave. Not because they didn't want to buy, but because they didn't feel seen. While there are always other reasons someone may not make a purchase, the goal is to eliminate "no service" as one of them.

Lesson from the Field

I was recently visiting stores with a regional manager when I saw a customer walk the entire sales floor—twice—passing three team members who never looked up. She left empty-handed. When we asked the staff if they'd noticed her, one said, "Oh yeah, she didn't look like she needed help." That wasn't just a missed sale—it was a missed connection, and likely a customer lost for good.

What stood out most was that this happened with a multi-unit leader in the store. If that's how the team behaves under leadership's watch, they likely don't believe they're doing anything wrong. That's why it's so important to understand what your team *believes* about serving customers—because until that mindset shifts, behavior won't either.

In high-performing stores, *foot traffic is treated like gold.* Every customer who walks through your doors is an opportunity, and it's your job to make sure it doesn't slip away.

What Great Leaders Do

No Customer Leaves Without an Interaction

Make it your team's mission: *Every customer gets acknowledged, engaged, assisted, and thanked.* That's not pressure—that's care.

Be Present Where Customers Are

Too often, team members disappear into the back room or get stuck doing tasks in dead zones. You can't engage customers from the stockroom. Position your team at key entry points, near high-interest products, or where customer flow naturally slows. Visibility increases approachability.

Watch for Browsing Behaviors

Someone who circles the same display twice, looks at sizes, or keeps glancing around—that's a buyer waiting for help. Train your team to *see* these cues—and act on them.

Revisit Hot Zones Regularly

The store flow constantly changes. During peak times, traffic hot spots emerge. Build habits around doing a visual "traffic scan" and adjusting team coverage accordingly—especially on weekends and evenings.

FINAL THOUGHT

Traffic means nothing without action—your team's presence, energy, and engagement are what turn footsteps into revenue.

TIME TO TAKE ACTION

Today, do a thirty-minute observation during a busy time. Don't step in—just watch.

- ☐ How many customers get a greeting but nothing more?
- ☐ How many browse for a few minutes and leave without a second interaction?

Then, huddle with the team immediately and reset expectations:

- ☐ Remind them not to let people drift. Greet them, then within two minutes, reengage.
- ☐ Real play if needed. Then, do a second thirty-minute pulse check later and compare.

DAY 11

Train the Team to Sell, Not Just Serve

FROM PASSIVE SERVICE TO PURPOSEFUL SELLING

Store teams should not just be order takers. They are there to proactively create value and drive sales. Equip your team members with the mindset and practical skills to move beyond passive service and become genuine solution providers. Train team members to listen for clues in the customer's response and body language. Uncover their needs and watch the magic happen.

This isn't about being "pushy"; it's about understanding customer needs deeply and confidently showcasing how your products and services enhance their lives, leading to higher average transactions and lasting customer relationships.

Lesson from the Field

I was filming a retail walk-through video at a high-end retail shop and observed a sales associate chat with a customer buying jeans and casually ask, "Do you need a belt to go with those? I love this one that just arrived." The customer paused, looked at the belt, and said, "Actually, yes!" That small, confident question turned a single-item sale into a full outfit—and a happier customer. We often assume that if the customer wanted it, they would have asked. But that assumption is dangerous and one that causes missed sales.

"Don't stop until the customer says, 'I am done.'"

—RACHEL WILLIAMSON

What Great Leaders Do

Shift the Mindset

The first step is to redefine the employee's role in their own eyes.

- ✓ Ask team members: "What's our ultimate goal when a customer walks in?" Guide the discussion from "helping customers" to "helping customers find solutions that they will purchase and be happy with."
- ✓ When discussing a product, train team members to focus on the *benefits* to the customer, not just the *features.*
- ✓ Teach team members that understanding a customer's *needs* (even unspoken ones) is the key to selling. What problem is

the customer trying to solve? How can our products provide the best solution?

Leverage Product Knowledge Beyond Features

Team members need to be product experts, but in a way that fuels sales.

- ✓ Instead of memorizing specs, have team members create short "stories" about products.
- ✓ Encourage physically demonstrating products. If it's a piece of apparel, have them explain how to style it. If it's electronics, show its key functions.
- ✓ Train on how your products stack up against competitors. This isn't about bad-mouthing but about confidently highlighting your unique selling propositions.
- ✓ Complete the look: For fashion, it's accessories. For electronics, it's cables or software. For home goods, it's cleaning supplies or complementary decor.
- ✓ If there's a limited-time offer, a new arrival, or a seasonal item, train team members to leverage it.

Real Playing and Ongoing Coaching

Theory without practice is often ineffective. Instead, use the daily huddle to practice a selling skill, real play customer interactions during downtime, and pair a new associate with a top-performing seller.

FINAL THOUGHT

We only have today to maximize the potential of each customer who walks through our doors. Every missed customer equals lost sales that we cannot get back. By implementing these strategies, you empower your retail team members to be proactive, informed, and confident salespeople who not only meet customer needs but also significantly contribute to the store's revenue.

TIME TO TAKE ACTION

- ☐ Teach your team that "every item has a friend" by selecting an item and asking them what item they could pair with it. It is a really fun activity that builds skills. Then observe them in action, reinforcing good performance and redirecting opportunities.

DAY 12

Lead from the Front

YOUR STORE DOESN'T RUN FROM THE BACK OFFICE—IT RUNS FROM THE SALES FLOOR

If you want to drive results, coach in real time, and lead your team to success, you need to be visible, engaged, and present where the action happens. While there may be tasks that need to be done in the back room, do them during low-traffic/low-sales periods. There might even be manager tasks that can be done right on the sales floor rather than in the back office.

Lesson from the Field

When I was a new store manager, I remember spending my first few weeks buried in the back office digging into reporting, convinced I was "running the business." Sales stayed flat. Then one Saturday, I decided to work entirely from the sales floor, helping customers, coaching associates in real time, and jumping in at the register during rushes. That day, sales hit the highest they had in months. More importantly, my team's energy was electric. I learned that the real work—and the real wins—happen out front, not behind a closed door.

The sales floor is your stage—it's where culture is built, customers are won, and performance is shaped. Leading from the front shows your team—and your customers—that you're all in. Leading from the front is how to drive real results.

What Great Leaders Do

The best retail leaders are visible, engaged, and actively part of the sales floor's daily rhythm. They aren't stuck in the back room, buried in emails, or poring over spreadsheets. Owning the sales floor isn't micromanaging; it's leading by example, fostering a dynamic environment, and directly influencing every interaction that drives results. Remember, customers, your team, and conversion are all on the sales floor!

Be Seen and Felt

✓ You're constantly circulating and observing, not just wandering.

- ✓ Move through different zones, watch customer flow, spot bottlenecks, and see which displays are working (or not).
- ✓ You're reading the room, sensing the store's energy: Is it bustling or slow? Are team members engaged or waiting? Your presence helps you gauge the store's pulse and react.
- ✓ Most importantly, your visible availability tells your team you're there for them. You're the go-to for overrides, tough customer issues, or quick product questions, empowering them to solve problems faster.

Moment of Truth

- ✓ Don't wait for weekly meetings. Give "in-the-moment" feedback.
- ✓ If an associate misses an add-on opportunity, a quick, private "pull-aside" is highly effective.
- ✓ Your presence helps you identify coaching opportunities in product knowledge, customer approach, or selling techniques. Turn potential missed sales into future successes.
- ✓ When an associate delivers exceptional service or makes a great sale, celebrate small wins publicly right away, perhaps with a high five or a shout-out. This quickly reinforces positive behaviors.

Remove Obstacles

Your presence helps you identify bottlenecks fast.

- ✓ Is the checkout slow? Displays messy? Fitting rooms unorganized? Address these before they impact sales or customer experience.
- ✓ Anticipate needs, scanning the floor for replenishment spots, overwhelmed team members, or struggling customers. Proactively offer assistance or direct resources where they're most needed.

✓ Finally, inventory and visual merchandising checks aren't passive. Ensure displays are stocked, clean, and appealing. If a key product is out of stock, you act immediately because, as my grandfather used to say, "You can't sell from an empty pushcart."

FINAL THOUGHT

By committing to a leadership style that is consistently visible and engaged on the sales floor, you transform yourself from a manager into a true sales leader. You inspire your team, enhance the customer experience, and directly contribute to the bottom line, proving that real results are indeed driven from the front.

Notes

TIME TO TAKE ACTION

- ☐ Spend the majority of your shift on the sales floor today, identifying opportunities and rewarding top performance.
- ☐ Find a way to get office work done during nonpeak times. Ask yourself, What benefit did I see from this behavior?

DAY 13

Handle Complaints like a Pro

EMPATHY, OWNERSHIP, ACCOUNTABILITY UNDER PRESSURE

Handling complaints is one of the most critical—and revealing—parts of retail leadership. It's not just about solving the immediate problem; it's about demonstrating empathy, ownership, and accountability under pressure.

Complaints aren't interruptions to the day—they're opportunities to turn disappointment into trust. When a customer brings you a concern, what they're really doing is giving ***you a second chance***. And when you handle it well, they often walk away feeling even better than if nothing had gone wrong at all.

This is where great stores separate themselves from average ones. In a great store, complaints are met with calm, quick action, and a desire to *make it right*, not just *make it go away*.

Lessons from the Field

Years ago, we had a customer storm into our store, furious about a sweater she had purchased. It had unraveled after one wash, and she was livid—not just about the product, but about how she felt dismissed during her earlier call to the store. She was yelling before I could even say hello. My first instinct was to go on the defensive—but instead, I paused, listened fully, and let her vent. I apologized sincerely—not with corporate speak, but with human empathy. I replaced the sweater, offered a discount on her next purchase, and then asked her for feedback on how we could improve. She softened almost immediately. By the end of our conversation, she was laughing, sharing stories about how much she normally loved shopping with us, and even thanked me for listening. She ended up buying two more sweaters before she left. More importantly, she became one of our most loyal customers—and even referred her friends.

That experience taught me a lesson I've carried throughout my career: When you meet frustration with empathy and ownership, even the worst situations can become your best opportunities.

What Great Leaders Do

Complaints: From Frustration to Loyalty

Every complaint is a crossroads. Handle it poorly, and you confirm the customer's worst fears about your brand. Handle it well, and you turn a moment of frustration into a story they'll proudly share. In retail, these moments aren't just transactions—they're trust tests. Pass them, and you earn loyalty that money can't buy.

Mindset Matters

- ✓ Treat every frustration as valid, regardless of fault. Focus on moving forward, not on proving who's right.
- ✓ Replace defensive language with solutions: "I understand your concern. Let's see how we can resolve this."
- ✓ Empower your team to fix common issues on the spot or escalate quickly.

Body Language and Communication

- ✓ Face customers, maintain appropriate eye contact, and use an open posture.
- ✓ Listen without interrupting, offering verbal affirmations and patience.
- ✓ Stay calm and speak evenly, even if the customer is agitated.
- ✓ Use warmth and reassurance—a genuine smile, friendly tone, and a sincere "I'm sorry" go a long way.

Act Fast

- ✓ Make resolving complaints the top priority.
- ✓ Know where to find answers quickly—policies, specs, contacts.
- ✓ Once a solution is found, act on it immediately.

FINAL THOUGHT

By consistently applying this framework and emphasizing the underlying principles of empathy, speed, and being solution focused, your team will transform complaint handling from a dreaded task into a powerful tool for building lasting customer loyalty.

TIME TO TAKE ACTION

Teach your team a simple, repeatable framework for handling complaints confidently and consistently. One example is the LAST method:

- ☐ **L**isten without interrupting.
- ☐ **A**pologize sincerely (even if you weren't personally responsible).
- ☐ **S**olve the issue quickly and fairly.
- ☐ **T**hank the customer for bringing it to your attention.

Practice it. Reinforce it in team huddles. Celebrate when team members recover from a poor experience and win the customer back.

Because in retail, complaint resolution isn't a soft skill—it's a core business driver.

DAY 14

Drive Repeat Business

TURN EVERY CUSTOMER INTO A LOYAL FAN

Loyal customers are your best marketing—and your most profitable ones. But loyalty doesn't happen by accident. It's earned one visit, one great interaction, one thoughtful follow-up at a time.

High-performing store leaders treat customer retention like a sales strategy, not an afterthought. They create systems that make follow-up part of the daily rhythm—not just a "nice to do."

Repeat business starts with relationship-building behavior, and you lead the way by recognizing and reinforcing it.

Lesson from the Field

I remember when a customer came into my store looking for a gift, and one of my team members took the time to ask a few extra questions and offer thoughtful suggestions. A week later, that same customer returned—this time with a friend—saying, "You made that so easy. I knew exactly where to come back when I needed another gift, and my friend needs one too."

One genuine interaction became two sales and a new loyal fan. A team that understands the importance of asking the right questions is invaluable to building lifelong customers and maximizing your store's revenue.

What Great Leaders Do

Repeat business doesn't come from gimmicks—it comes from *trust*. Customers return because their last visit made them feel something: valued, impressed, and excited to come back. Loyalty is built on consistency, care, and excellence in every corner of the store.

Here's how top-performing stores earn repeat visits:

Nail the Basics, Every Time

- ✓ Offer warm, helpful service. People return to places where they feel welcome, not rushed or ignored.
- ✓ Maintain a clean, organized store. A clean store communicates pride, safety, and professionalism. Customers notice when you care, especially clean fitting rooms and windows, and all lights lit!

- ✓ Ensure a relevant, well-merchandised assortment. Stay in tune with what your customer wants. Surprise them with newness. Make sure sizes and styles are available and accessible.
- ✓ Use speed and ease. From fitting room to checkout, a smooth experience matters.

Build Relationships, Not Just Transactions

- ✓ Engage in meaningful ways. Ask questions. Learn names. Remember preferences. Show you care.
- ✓ Offer to call customers when new products come in, when markdowns occur, or when you reset the sales floor. The key is, once you offer, do it! We lose trust when we offer to call and then never do.
- ✓ Capture contact info thoughtfully. Train team members to offer sign-up as a *benefit*, not a pitch.
- ✓ Use contact info wisely. Don't just blast promotions. Share value—new drops, styling tips, exclusive invites.
- ✓ One stylist started texting thank-you notes to her clients with product tips and her clientele jumped 20 percent.

Follow Through with Excellence

- ✓ No matter the day, time, or who's on shift, every customer should feel the same level of care.
- ✓ Handle returns, sizing issues, or questions with grace and professionalism. A well-managed hiccup is often *more* memorable than a smooth transaction.
- ✓ Offer surprise and delight moments. These don't have to be big. A handwritten thank-you note, offering to hold a favorite item, or simply remembering what they bought last time goes a long way.

FINAL THOUGHT

Driving repeat business isn't about chasing customers—it's about *earning them.*

When your store is clean, your service is warm, your assortment is right, and your follow-up is personal, customers return naturally—because they trust that your store will deliver, again and again.

Notes

TIME TO TAKE ACTION

Run a "customer love" campaign:

1. Pick three team members to do personal outreach today—a thank-you text, product arrival alert, or friendly follow-up.
2. At the next team huddle, share who did it, how the customer responded, and what resulted. Make it visible. Make it part of your culture.
3. Audit your customer email list. Are team members capturing emails or phone numbers during checkout, or skipping it? Coach them to position it as a benefit ("We'll let you know first when new styles drop!"), not a favor.

Power in the Pause

WEEK 2 RECAP: DRIVING SALES THROUGH SERVICE AND STANDARDS

This week shifted the spotlight from *you* to your *store*. The focus? Creating consistent, high-performance customer experiences and driving revenue through effective leadership on the floor.

Focus Areas

Day 8—Make Exceptional Customer Service Nonnegotiable

Great service isn't optional—it's your competitive edge. Set the standard, model it daily, and hold the line.

Day 9—KPIs and Behaviors That Drive Results

Know your numbers—but more importantly, coach the behaviors that impact them. Data is only useful when it leads to action.

Day 10—Maximize Traffic

Every person who walks through your door is an opportunity. Don't count traffic—*convert it.*

Day 11—Train Team Members to Sell, Not Just Serve

Service is about making people feel good. Selling is about solving problems. Teach your team to do both with confidence.

Day 12—Own the Sales Floor

Visibility is power. Great leaders lead from the front, coaching in real time and driving momentum where it matters most.

Day 13—Handle Complaints like a Pro

Every complaint is a second chance. Listen, own it, and recover in a way that earns trust—and loyalty.

Day 14—Drive Repeat Business

The sale isn't over at the register. Create experiences that bring customers back again and again.

REFLECT AND RESET

Where did you see the biggest improvement in customer experience or sales this week?

Which KPI do you need to track more intentionally?

What service standard do you want to reinforce in Week 3?

RACHEL-*ism*

When service and selling come together, stores thrive—and so do teams.

WEEK 3

Develop an Unstoppable Team

Day 15: Hire for Attitude, Train for Skill

Day 16: Onboard with Purpose

Day 17: Train, Don't Just Tell

Day 18: Delegate and Empower

Day 19: Give Constructive Feedback Regularly

Day 20: Identify and Develop Future Leaders

Day 21: Recognize and Celebrate Wins

Recap: Power in the Pause

REAL WINS, REAL LESSONS

When I stepped into the role at Ann Taylor in City Center Mall back in the 1990s, the store *looked* like it was thriving—sales numbers were solid, and top team members were competitive and hungry. There were sales team members who were each selling over $1 million annually. The regional manager who hired me officed from the back room. So, expectations were high and standards even higher.

But underneath that surface was something else entirely. Something you had to experience working on the sales floor day in and day out.

- ✓ Team members *rushed* to greet customers first, even cutting each other off.
- ✓ Returns turned into *battles*, with team members getting visibly upset if the return hit their paycheck.
- ✓ Tension was high. Trust was low. Customers felt it. And, so did I.

I saw customers peering around the corner looking into the store. I asked what they were looking for and they said they had a return and didn't want to come in if their salesperson was working as they felt guilt if they brought something back. Oy vey. It was clear. *We had a culture problem, one rooted in an outdated commission structure.*

So, we started to address what we could until the structure was changed at corporate.

First, I held a meeting and called out the elephant in the room:

"We've created a system that rewards individual wins, but it's costing us the customer experience. Beyond that, we aren't operating as a team, and the store is not reaching its sales targets." We worked together to align on what we owned in our behavior and how to leverage the team to grow the business.

I spoke to headquarters about what didn't work, and eventually, the commission structure changed for the better. But until it did, we had to set clear expectations on what would be acceptable behavior and how to grow the business and grow together as a team.

- ✓ We introduced *shared goals*, winning as a team.
- ✓ We shifted language from "my customer" to "our customer."
- ✓ We trained the team on service recovery and how to turn a return into a relationship.
- ✓ We grew our service offering, visiting customers' homes to assess their closet and curate a wardrobe they loved. No retailers were offering this, and our business skyrocketed, giving our sales associates a steady stream of customers.

It wasn't easy. Some resisted—afraid they'd lose income, afraid of change. Some left the business.

But slowly, we saw the shift:

- ✓ Team members began *helping* each other close sales.
- ✓ Fitting rooms became active zones of engagement.
- ✓ No one panicked when a return walked in—they focused on what the customer needed next.
- ✓ Energy on the floor changed. So did customer feedback.

And in the months that followed, we didn't just *match* our old numbers—we beat them. Consistently. With less drama, stronger morale, and better customer loyalty.

Lesson Learned

Commission can drive performance—but without the right leadership and structure, it can kill culture.

When we realigned incentives to reward collaboration and customer experience, *everyone won.*

DAY 15

Hire for Attitude, Train for Skill

YOU CAN TRAIN ALMOST ANYTHING—EXCEPT ATTITUDE

A positive mindset, strong work ethic, and team-first mentality can't be taught—they're either there or they're not. Skills can be developed, but the right attitude is what fuels great service, team morale, and long-term success. What do you do if you have the wrong attitudes? Don't just accept it. Have conversations to address the challenges, listen without judgment, and be clear on what is expected.

Don't settle for warm bodies. Hire people who show up with energy, curiosity, and a willingness to learn. That's the foundation of a winning team.

Lesson from the Field

One of my clients had their team start each shift with a mindset reset. Things like positive affirmations and even striking the Superman pose to get in the right headspace. I loved it. And I watched it work in what could have been a tough selling environment. The energy was contagious.

The bottom line? You can't afford to hire what Jon Gordon calls "energy vampires"—the ones who suck the life out of your store, your business, and your team. Culture is built one shift, one mindset, one hire at a time. Do what works to protect it.

> ***"Worried another store in the mall will recruit your well-trained team members away? It's no reason to skip the training. It will be worse if they stay, never get trained, and scare your customers away."***
>
> **—RACHEL WILLIAMSON**

What Great Leaders Do

A single hire can shift your store's energy—for better or worse. You've likely felt the difference. One employee with a positive mindset, a relentless work ethic, and a willingness to learn can elevate an entire team. But one with a poor attitude—even with years of experience—can drag down morale, spark drama, and drive customers away.

That's why hiring for attitude is nonnegotiable. Skill can be taught. A good outlook? Much harder to instill.

I was a recruiter for a year at Bath & Body Works before I became a district manager. I remember interviewing a candidate with zero retail experience—but she radiated positivity and asked smart, curious questions. We took a chance, and within weeks, she was outselling seasoned team members and lifting everyone's energy. She was eventually promoted to a manager role and ran a very successful store. It was a reminder: You can teach the register, but you can't teach heart. And when you bring a top performer to the team, everyone else steps up!

Hire for the Long Game

Don't get dazzled by a polished résumé. Experience in retail doesn't always translate to success—especially if it comes with bad habits or a fixed mindset. Instead, look for curiosity, humility, energy, and grit.

Ask Behavior-Based Questions

The following questions uncover whether someone can grow with you or become a barrier:

- ✓ How do you handle being wrong?
- ✓ Tell me about a time you received hard feedback—what did you do with it?
- ✓ What does great service mean to you?

Prioritize Culture Add, Not Just Culture Fit

You're not looking for clones—you're looking for people who make the team better. Do they lift others? Own their shift? Solve problems with customers instead of making excuses?

Teach the Mechanics, Coach the Mindset

- ✓ Yes, they need to learn how to process a return or set a table.
- ✓ What really drives results is how they *show up*—on a rainy Tuesday, when they're tired, or when there's a line out the door. That's why the real training never stops.

Build a Reputation as a Place People Grow

When you celebrate people not just for tenure but for transformation—when you reward hustle, ownership, and good energy—you create a team others want to join. That's your hiring pipeline.

FINAL THOUGHT

Retail is a people-first business. When you hire people who care, everything else becomes easier: service improves, teams collaborate, sales follow. The right hire isn't the one with the most experience. It's the one with the right heart, the right hustle, and the right attitude.

Notes

TIME TO TAKE ACTION

- ☐ During your next interview, give the candidate a real-life scenario from your store and ask how they would handle it. Watch for signs of positivity, ownership, and curiosity in their response. Then, ask them to real play a customer interaction—you'll learn more in five minutes of play than from fifty rehearsed answers.

DAY 16

Onboard with Purpose

KEEP YOUR TALENT AROUND

Did you know that a new hire's first thirty days determine their success? The initial days and weeks of a new employee's journey are pivotal. No onboarding or poorly completed onboarding results in 30 percent of new hires quitting within the first ninety days. Continually hiring and onboarding new team members costs thousands of dollars per employee. These are all compelling reasons to ensure every new hire has a wonderful onboarding experience.

Lesson from the Field

I often hear nightmare stories of retail brands with over 100 percent turnover! I remember one seasonal employee who almost quit after her first week. No one had shown her where anything was, and she spent every shift guessing. After the store slowed down, they assigned her a "buddy" and walked her through the expectations; she became one of their strongest performers. That experience taught me that onboarding isn't extra—it's everything.

A well-structured onboarding program—or a thoughtfully implemented alternative when a formal program is absent—lays the groundwork for their success, fosters a sense of belonging, and ultimately contributes to a thriving retail operation.

What Great Leaders Do

Power of Effective Onboarding

Beyond simply completing paperwork, true onboarding is about integrating new team members into the company culture, equipping them with the necessary tools and knowledge, and empowering them to contribute quickly and confidently.

The Results of Effective Onboarding, According to Research

- ✓ Employees who feel supported and engaged from day one are far more likely to stay for the long haul. Strong onboarding isn't just a nice-to-have—it's your first step toward higher retention and a stronger team.

- ✓ When new team members clearly understand their roles, expectations, and available resources, they become productive faster.
- ✓ Feeling valued and connected from the start boosts morale and strengthens employee commitment.
- ✓ Confident and well-trained employees are better equipped to deliver an exceptional customer experience.
- ✓ Onboarding is a powerful opportunity to reinforce your company's values, mission, and unique brand culture.

In-House Onboarding Program

If you have a company onboarding program, be the manager who doesn't just go through the motions. Embrace the program fully and personalize it where you can.

No Formal Onboarding Available

It's your chance to build something meaningful—even a simple plan can make a big difference.

- ✓ Before their first day, make sure the new hire knows where to park, what to bring, and what to expect—and ensure the team is prepped, the schedule is set, and their tools are ready.
- ✓ Make the first day feel special by introducing them to the team, touring the store, and sharing the mission behind the work.
- ✓ Start with low-pressure tasks so they can ease into the role while getting a feel for how things operate.
- ✓ Assign a go-to person who can answer questions and help them feel supported from the start.

FINAL THOUGHT

The best onboarding doesn't stop after week one. Use daily huddles, product trainings, real-playing, and regular feedback to keep new hires learning and growing.

TIME TO TAKE ACTION

- ☐ Audit your onboarding process. Are new hires set up for success?
- ☐ Talk to your most recent hire. What was their experience like? What would they change? It is never too late to go back and retrain a new hire who might have had a less-than-optimal initial onboarding experience.

DAY 17

Train, Don't Just Tell

TELLING SOMEONE WHAT TO DO ISN'T TRAINING—*SHOWING* THEM IS

Hands-on, real-time training builds confidence, consistency, and competence. Verbal instructions alone fade fast, but when someone sees it done, does it themself, and gets immediate feedback, they learn it for life. Great leaders don't just delegate—they *develop*. If you want your team to execute with excellence, invest the time to train them the right way.

Lesson from the Field

A new associate once told me she had no idea how to greet customers. She had been told what to say, but no one had ever shown her how to say it with confidence. We practiced a few real-play scenarios, and by the end of the week, she was greeting like a pro. That's when I realized: telling creates confusion, but training builds capability.

A greeting is more than a "hello"—it's the first step in winning a customer's trust. If you want that moment to feel warm, personal, and genuine, it can't be left to chance. Every role, even greeting, deserves training—because every moment with a customer is a chance to make your brand unforgettable.

"Tell me and I forget; teach me and I may remember; involve me and I learn."

—BENJAMIN FRANKLIN

What Great Leaders Do

The fundamental difference between "telling" and "training" lies in empowerment and long-term capability building. Telling is a one-way directive; training is a collaborative process that equips your team members to succeed independently.

Demonstrate, Don't Just Describe

Visual demonstration clarifies expectations immediately. It reduces misinterpretation and provides a tangible example to follow.

Explain the "Why," Not Just the "What"

Understanding the reason behind a task increases engagement, buy-in, and the likelihood of consistent execution. It shifts the task from a chore to a meaningful contribution.

Facilitate Practice and Repetition

Practical application in a safe environment builds confidence and muscle memory. It allows for immediate feedback and correction before high-stakes situations arise.

Provide Specific, Constructive Feedback

Generic criticism is demotivating and unhelpful. Specific feedback, focused on actions and their impact, provides clear pathways for improvement.

Encourage Questions and Active Listening

This approach ensures comprehension, addresses potential roadblocks proactively, and fosters a safe environment where team members feel comfortable admitting when they don't understand something.

Delegate with Support, Not Just Assignment

Delegation with built-in support mechanisms shows trust while still offering a safety net. It allows team members to own tasks and develop problem-solving skills.

FINAL THOUGHT

By consistently applying these principles, you'll transform your store from a place where tasks are merely dictated to one where team members are actively developed, leading to higher performance, greater job satisfaction, and a more resilient, high-impact store.

TIME TO TAKE ACTION

- ☐ Choose one selling skill and do a hands-on training session today. This should be done during slow periods so as not to take away from the customer experience.

DAY 18

Delegate and Empower

IF YOU TRY TO DO EVERYTHING YOURSELF, YOU'LL BURN OUT—AND HOLD YOUR TEAM BACK

Great leaders don't just *do*—they *develop*. Delegation isn't about dumping tasks; it's about giving team members the chance to grow, contribute, and take ownership.

When you empower others, you build trust, expand your bench strength, and free yourself up to focus on what matters most. Let go of control so your team can step up.

Lesson from the Field

Early in my career, I worked for small, independent retailers. We ran on minimum payroll and I was the kind of store manager who was accustomed to doing everything myself. I set the floor, solved the problems, and made every decision because I thought that's what great leaders did. My team was dependable, but they rarely took initiative. One day, I realized I wasn't giving them the chance. So, I made a shift. I started asking questions instead of giving answers: "How would you merchandise this table to drive sell-through?" or "What's your plan for getting shipments out today?" To my surprise, they stepped up—offering ideas, taking ownership, and showing leadership I hadn't seen before. That was a turning point for me. I stopped trying to be the smartest person in the room and started focusing on drawing out the strengths of others. The store didn't just run better—it became better, because we were growing leaders, not just completing tasks.

> ***"Surround yourself with great people, delegate authority, and get out of the way."***
>
> **—RONALD REAGAN**

What Great Leaders Do

Delegating and empowering are about strategically entrusting tasks and decision-making authority to your team, fostering ownership and growth. Trying to be a superhero store manager who does everything leads to failure and makes it difficult to show your boss that you can handle more responsibility.

Assign Tasks with Clear Outcomes, Not Just Actions

When assigning tasks, focus on clear outcomes rather than just actions. For example, rather than saying, "Clean up the back room," try, "Please organize the back room so all incoming shipments are staged for efficient processing by opening tomorrow." This helps your team understand the purpose behind the task and what success looks like.

Provide the "Why" and the "What If"

Explain the objective and parameters for independent decision-making.

Trust, but Verify

This means you "trust" the person to complete the task, but you still circle back and ask if they have questions or need anything.

Encourage "Problem-Solving" over "Reporting Problems"

Push them to think critically and propose solutions before coming to you.

Celebrate Initiative and Learning

Acknowledge and praise independent action, even if the outcome isn't perfect, focusing on the effort and learning.

FINAL THOUGHT

When you *delegate and empower*, you're not just offloading tasks; you're cultivating a team of self-reliant leaders who are invested in the store's success. Great leaders don't hoard tasks. They develop people by giving away responsibility with accountability.

TIME TO TAKE ACTION

- ☐ Delegation is a leadership muscle—and today's the day to flex it. Think about one task you routinely handle that could (and should) be owned by someone on your team.
- ☐ Identify the right person, explain the desired outcome, and hand it off with clarity and trust.
- ☐ Then—don't forget—circle back to check progress.

DAY 19

Give Constructive Feedback Regularly

FEEDBACK ISN'T OPTIONAL—IT'S A LEADERSHIP RESPONSIBILITY

If your team only hears from you when something goes wrong, you're missing the mark—and so are they. High-performing teams grow through clear, consistent, and constructive feedback—not guesswork or assumptions.

Feedback isn't criticism—it's a commitment to your team's success. When delivered well, it builds trust, sharpens skills, and drives accountability.

Lesson from the Field

As a young store manager, I struggled to give feedback—I worried it would hurt relationships and they might quit or, even worse, not like me. One afternoon, I noticed a team member missing key steps in a greeting. Instead of waiting for a formal review, I pulled her aside gently. I observed the greeting. I focused on what she did well and gave one clear tip to improve. She thanked me and told me it was the first time anyone had taken the time to help her get better. Her confidence soared, her greetings improved, and sales followed. That moment taught me: Feedback isn't criticism—it's care in action.

The best feedback is immediate, specific, and actionable. It happens in real time, not weeks later. It focuses on behaviors, not personalities. And it always answers the question: *What can I do differently to improve?*

Great leaders don't shy away from tough conversations. They lean in with clarity, compassion, and the belief that everyone can get better. One of my favorite recent reads, *Difficult Conversations Don't Have to Be Difficult* by Jon Gordon and Amy P. Kelly, offers a simple, effective model for addressing tough topics with empathy while preserving relationships.

Your team deserves to know how they're doing—and how to get to the next level. Don't make them guess.

What Great Leaders Do

Regular, constructive feedback is a continuous dialogue, not an annual event. It's about catching moments for growth and celebrating small wins, building a culture of transparency and improvement.

Give Feedback in the Moment

- ✓ Address behavior—positive or corrective—within minutes or hours, not days or weeks.
- ✓ Use calm, clear language that focuses on actions, not personal traits.
- ✓ Pull team members aside respectfully and make feedback part of everyday coaching, not a big event.
- ✓ The Situation-Behavior-Impact (SBI) model works well because the structured approach provides clear context and factual observation, and explains the consequence, leading to better understanding and a higher likelihood of behavioral change.
- ✓ Offer one or two clear next steps so the person knows how to improve or repeat the behavior. It works because the feedback is directly tied to the event, making it easier for the team member to connect the behavior with the outcome and apply the learning immediately.

Have the Conversation, Even If You Dread It

- ✓ As hard as conversations can be, when we tell the truth, we get better together.
- ✓ Assume positive intent. Do not take it personally. Manage emotional energy. No personal attacks.
- ✓ Respect your team member and the process.
- ✓ Relationships matter most.

Create a Culture of Growth, Not Fear

- ✓ Balance feedback with encouragement, showing belief in each person's potential.
- ✓ Welcome feedback in return—modeling that everyone, including you, is still learning.
- ✓ Normalize feedback as a tool for development, not discipline.

FINAL THOUGHT

Constructive feedback is not a one-time event but a continuous, collaborative conversation that fuels growth. By delivering timely, specific, and balanced feedback—and by listening as much as you speak—you create an environment where improvement is welcomed, strengths are celebrated, and every team member feels supported to reach their full potential. When feedback becomes a daily habit rather than a dreaded task, your team's performance and confidence will soar.

Notes

TIME TO TAKE ACTION

- ☐ Pick one team member today and give them real-time, constructive feedback using this three-part formula:

    1. **What you observed**—"I noticed you..."
    2. **Why it matters**—"This impacts the team/customer because..."
    3. **How to improve—"Next time, try..."**

- ☐ Then, set a ten-minute block at the end of your shift to reflect: Did you give feedback today? If not, who needs it tomorrow?

DAY 20

Identify and Develop Future Leaders

TOMORROW'S STORE LEADERS ARE ON YOUR FLOOR TODAY

Strong stores are built by strong leaders—and those leaders don't just appear out of nowhere. They're already on your floor, folding denim, checking in shipments, helping customers, and watching how *you* lead.

Here's the truth: The best leaders don't wait until someone is "ready." They spot the spark, the hunger, the hustle—and they fan the flame. They coach, stretch, and challenge their team members *before* they have the title.

Lesson from the Field

I remember one young woman I hired during the holiday rush—no retail experience, but she worked the floor like she'd been there for years. One Saturday, with a staffing shortage and peak traffic, she took charge without a title: organized the team, kept the floor covered, and never missed a customer. I started giving her stretch assignments, and within a year, she was running her own store. Great leaders don't wait for a title—they lead where they are.

If you want a store that thrives long-term, you have to think like a talent scout. Who's showing ownership? Who's hungry to learn? Who's stepping up without being asked? The future of your store—and maybe even your company—depends on your ability to grow the next generation of leadership.

Great leaders aren't just great operators. They're talent builders. And your bench strength tomorrow depends on what you do today.

What Great Leaders Do

Look for Initiative, Not Just Tenure

Leadership isn't about how long someone's been around. It's about attitude and action. Notice who jumps in without being asked, supports teammates naturally, solves problems on the fly, and cares about the store like it's their own.

Start Small, Then Stretch

Give team members opportunities to lead in small ways. Ask them to run a daily huddle, mentor a new hire, or take ownership of a key zone or product category. These "leader moments" reveal their readiness—and build their confidence.

Coach in Real Time

When the store is quiet or a teachable moment presents itself, pull them aside. Talk through a decision you made, explain a KPI, or let them help solve a floor challenge. These real-time conversations are where leadership is born.

Connect the Dots

Help your future leaders think beyond tasks. Show them how staffing drives sales, how merchandising influences traffic flow, and how greeting every customer impacts conversion. Help them see the big picture and how their role fits into it.

Map the Path Forward

Check in regularly. Ask them what they want next—and share what it takes to get there. Be specific about the behaviors and results they need to demonstrate. Let them know you're in their corner.

Celebrate the Climb

Growth is rarely linear. Progress is the goal. When you see a team member step up, take initiative, or demonstrate leadership, recognize it. Celebrate effort as much as outcome.

FINAL THOUGHT

Leadership development doesn't start with a title—it starts with trust, opportunity, and belief. Invest in your people, and your bench will always be strong.

Notes

TIME TO TAKE ACTION

- ☐ Identify one team member with leadership potential and begin actively mentoring them. Schedule a one-on-one to learn about their career goals, strengths, and areas they want to develop. From there, co-create a growth plan that includes small leadership opportunities—like running a huddle, mentoring a peer, or leading a floor set.
- ☐ Check in weekly to provide feedback, coaching, and encouragement. Your investment now could shape your store's next great leader.

DAY 21

Recognize and Celebrate Wins

WHAT GETS RECOGNIZED GETS REPEATED

Recognition isn't just a "nice to have"—it's a leadership tool that builds confidence, loyalty, and momentum. When team members feel seen and appreciated, they bring more energy, effort, and pride to their work. Celebrating wins—big and small—shows your team that what they do matters. And that's what keeps morale high and performance strong.

Lesson from the Field

I once had a quiet team member who rarely spoke up—but after a big weekend, I called out her flawless execution on reworking the clearance area during a team huddle. The smile that lit up her face was unforgettable—and from that day on, her confidence (and performance) soared. A little recognition turned into a lot of impact.

> ***"What gets recognized gets reinforced, and what gets reinforced gets repeated."***
>
> **—ANONYMOUS**

What Great Leaders Do

Catch Them Doing Something Right

This is perhaps the most impactful form of recognition because it's real-time and directly tied to desired behaviors, whether on the sales floor, during merchandising, or working in the back room.

Shout-Out Board/Appreciation Station

- ✓ Create a visible, public platform for recognition. A whiteboard in the break room where managers and even peers can write specific thank-you notes.
- ✓ Utilize an internal communication app or a dedicated recognition platform where managers can post achievements and team members can react and add their congratulations.

- ✓ Start each shift or morning huddle with a quick round of "wins" from the previous day.

Celebrate Milestones

- ✓ Recognize not just individual actions, but also sustained effort, tenure, and team achievements.
- ✓ Acknowledge work anniversaries with a small card, a verbal thank-you, or even a preferred coffee gift card.
- ✓ When the team hits a daily, weekly, or monthly sales goal:
  - ▹ **Small Wins:** Bring in bagels or coffee for the morning shift.
  - ▹ **Medium Wins:** Order pizza for lunch, or organize a gift card raffle for achieving a specific target.
  - ▹ **Big Wins** (e.g., hitting quarterly goals)**:** Plan a team outing (bowling, mini golf), a catered lunch, or a small bonus/gift for everyone if company policy allows.
- ✓ Share positive customer reviews or comments with the entire team, specifically calling out individuals mentioned.

One-on-One Appreciation

- ✓ Sometimes the most meaningful recognition happens in a private conversation.
- ✓ A manager can offer a simple, heartfelt thank-you card acknowledging a specific effort or achievement.
- ✓ Have a brief, informal conversation with an employee where you express appreciation.
- ✓ Sometimes, the best recognition is showing an employee you value their opinion and want to invest in their growth.

Team Celebration Events

- ✓ Build camaraderie and celebrate collective success. Here are some ideas:

- A holiday potluck/party is a fun way to celebrate the season and the team's hard work throughout the year.
- Plan a team-building outing purely for fun and team bonding, acknowledging collective efforts.
- Celebrate other important aspects of retail success, such as achieving a perfect inventory count, acing a compliance audit, or successfully onboarding a new technology system.

FINAL THOUGHT

By implementing these practical recognition strategies, a retail store manager can create a positive, appreciative, and highly motivated team that feels valued and, in turn, works harder and contributes to the store's overall success.

Notes

TIME TO TAKE ACTION

- ☐ Find one team member doing something great today and praise them publicly.

Power in the Pause

WEEK 3 RECAP: BUILDING AND ELEVATING YOUR TEAM

This week was all about people. The best store leaders don't just manage a team—they build one. From hiring to recognition, you focused on how to attract, grow, and retain top talent.

Week 3 Focus Areas

Day 15—Hire for Attitude, Train for Skill

Skills can be taught. A great attitude, curiosity, and work ethic? Those are your nonnegotiables.

Day 16—Onboard with Purpose

The first days shape long-term success. Start with clarity, consistency, and connection to the brand and role.

Day 17—Train, Don't Just Tell

Telling is instruction. Training is transformation. Set your team up for success through hands-on learning and real-time coaching.

Day 18—Delegate and Empower

Leadership isn't about doing everything—it's about trusting others to rise. Empower your team to take ownership.

Day 19—Give Constructive Feedback Regularly

Feedback should be timely, specific, and rooted in helping others grow. Make it a daily leadership habit—not a once-a-year event.

Day 20—Identify and Develop Future Leaders

Look for potential, not perfection. Mentor your high performers, stretch their skills, and invest in their growth.

Day 21—Recognize and Celebrate Wins

Appreciation fuels motivation. Celebrate effort and achievement—because what gets recognized gets repeated.

REFLECT AND RESET

Who stood out on your team this week—and why?

What development opportunity can you create for a future leader?

How will you keep the momentum going into next week?

> ***"Great stores aren't built by chance—they're built by great teams. And great teams are built by you."***
>
> **—RACHEL WILLIAMSON**

WEEK 4

Master Operational Excellence

REAL WINS, REAL LESSONS

*I was in the first six months of being a new store man-*ager at the Gap, and it was the highest-volume location I had ever led to date. Looking back, I loved that store. The team was incredible, and we were riding a wave of explosive growth. Every day was fast-paced and fun—the kind of challenge that made me feel fully alive.

As Black Friday approached, my district manager, Bill, came in to help me prepare for my first big holiday weekend in this role. As we walked through the operational plan, he said something that sounded simple enough: "Take Wednesday's deposit and buy change for the weekend."

You got it, I thought. No problem. I didn't want to sound stupid, so I didn't ask questions; I took the instructions at face value.

So, I headed to the bank with the store's full deposit in hand. When I told the banker I needed to exchange it all for change, her eyes widened. This wasn't a couple hundred dollars per register. I was asking for over $10,000 in coins and small bills. They didn't even have that much change on-site. The bank had to courier money in from another location just to fulfill my request.

When the bank called, we took our shipment dolly to pick up the change. I returned to the store with a dolly stacked high with coin boxes and strapped-down bill packs. We wheeled it through the mall like we were transporting a miniature armored truck. The whole thing barely fit in the safe—and by "barely," I mean we had to rearrange everything to make it work, including the locked drawers.

Every morning and every night, we spent close to an hour counting that change.

It was tedious. It was ridiculous. And it was, in hindsight, hilarious. Eventually, my team and I looked at each other and said, "This *cannot* be what Bill meant."

And, of course, it wasn't.

Bill had assumed I'd understand that he meant a reasonable amount of change to keep the registers moving—maybe a few hundred dollars per drawer. I, on the other hand, took his direction quite literally. And because I didn't ask any clarifying questions, I made an unnecessary mountain out of small bills.

Afterward, we all had a good laugh about it. Bill learned to give more precise instructions.

And I learned a leadership lesson that has stayed with me ever since:

Clear communication isn't just helpful—it's everything.

At the Gap, I learned how to run a tight, high-performing operation. But that Black Friday weekend taught me something just as important: When in doubt, ask. Assume nothing. The smallest miscommunication can create a whole lot of unnecessary effort.

And sometimes, that effort looks like wheeling $10,000 in change through the mall.

DAY 22

Scheduling for Productivity

SMART SCHEDULING = HIGHER SALES, BETTER SERVICE, AND A HAPPIER TEAM

Scheduling isn't just plugging names into a grid—it's one of the most powerful levers a retail leader has to drive performance. The right schedule maximizes revenue, elevates service, reduces burnout, and helps your team win. The wrong one? It creates chaos, crushes morale, wastes money (profit), and leaves sales on the table.

High-performing managers treat the schedule like a strategy document. They staff to traffic, not just hours. They match the right people to the right shifts. They plan for peak volume with their strongest sellers and ensure that coverage supports both the customer experience and operational flow. It's not about fairness. It's about effectiveness.

Who's working matters. When they're working, it matters more.

Lesson from the Field

When I was the director of store operations at Limited Too and Justice, every location was still handwriting schedules. I pitched a scheduling solution to the CEO, but he shot it down, insisting all store traffic patterns were "the same." So, I thought it would help to share what I was seeing. I pulled traffic patterns for every single store and built a 580-page slide deck. We walked through the deck together. By slide ninety, he looked at me and asked, "Do you have every store in here?" "I sure do," I replied. He finally agreed, and we rolled out Matrix Retail scheduling. That first year, we saved over $5 million in payroll—without cutting a single hour—by aligning labor with traffic and making sure our strongest sellers were in the right place at the right time.

> ***"Right people, right place, right time will give you the right outcome, every time."***
>
> **—RACHEL WILLIAMSON**

What Great Leaders Do

The best store leaders constantly evaluate labor through one lens: how to drive revenue and elevate the customer experience.

Align Talent to Traffic

- ✓ Evaluate your business, identifying peak days/hours.
- ✓ Match the peaks to your team's availability. Look at your top talent. Can they work when the business needs them most?

- ✓ Identify the shifts you need but cannot fill today.
- ✓ Meet with each team member and let them know what you need. They may be able to make adjustments to their availability. If they cannot, hiring top talent becomes job number one.
- ✓ Schedule your strongest floor supervisors during peak hours to maximize performance. A leader should always be on the floor in those windows—coaching, supporting, and shifting priorities in real time.

Build a Productivity Mindset

- ✓ Now that the right people are working at the right time, instill a productivity mindset. Not just in your managers, but in every member of the team. They all play a role in exceeding sales targets.
- ✓ Set clear microgoals for every shift. Let the team know the goals and what you need from them during your daily huddles.
- ✓ Cross-train team members regularly and rotate responsibilities to increase engagement and reduce fatigue.
- ✓ Protect time before and after peak hours for product replenishment, visual resets, or operational tasks. Idle hands during traffic—or tasking during prime sales windows—cost revenue.

FINAL THOUGHT

Smart scheduling isn't just about having "enough people"—it's about having *the right people, in the right place, at the right time, doing the right work.* When every shift is built with purpose, productivity goes up, stress goes down, and both customers and team members win. Your schedule is a strategy—treat it like one.

TIME TO TAKE ACTION

- ☐ With every schedule you write, ask: Are our peak hours covered with our top performers?
- ☐ Revisit your traffic patterns weekly and rotate responsibilities so your most trained team members are front and center when the stakes are high. This is not a "once and done" activity—it's a weekly leadership habit.

DAY 23

Merchandising for Sales Impact

WHERE STRATEGY MEETS STORYTELLING ON THE SALES FLOOR

Merchandising is more than folding tables or moving fixtures—it's a conversation with your customer. Done right, it drives sales, elevates the experience, and keeps people coming back. Great leaders know merchandising blends product, storytelling, and strategy. Every display must inspire purchase.

Many brands demand strict planogram compliance—but when sizes break or items sell out, the display falls flat. That's when strong leaders step in to reimagine the space, keep it fresh, and drive sales.

Fast door-to-floor flow, right sizing, and curated product stories are core to success. Too often, broken sizes pile up, mannequins wear what's not for sale, and endcaps sit empty while back rooms overflow. That's not just messy—it's costly.

Merchandising is a daily, intentional act—adapting constantly to traffic, inventory, and marketing. Every item should be shoppable, sized right, and part of a bigger story that makes customers say "yes." Your floor is your silent seller—make it a powerful one.

Lesson from the Field

When I managed a high-volume flagship, I once found the main feature rack filled with only two sizes of a bestselling jacket—small and XXL—while medium and large were out back. The display looked full, but customers left frustrated. After fixing the sizing mix and telling the product story clearly, that jacket became one of our top sellers that week. It was a simple fix that made a huge impact—proof that merchandising is about more than looks. As a high-ticket item, it also elevated our average order value, which helped us make our day faster!

"Your merchandising is your silent salesperson. Make sure it's saying the right thing."

—RACHEL WILLIAMSON

What Great Leaders Do

Not all retail brands provide clear, ongoing direction for maintaining visual merchandising, especially as product sells through. When inventory shifts, replace empty or broken displays with full-size assortments to keep the presentation shoppable. Featuring out-of-stock items frustrates customers and disrupts the experience.

If you have specific brand guidelines, follow them closely. If not, use the points below to create a visually appealing, sales-driving store that reflects pride and intention.

Create Clear Focal Points That Sell

- ✓ Use high-traffic areas (front table, power wall, endcaps) to highlight key items.
- ✓ Tell a product story—why now, why this, why them.
- ✓ Feature high-margin, seasonal, or high-inventory items prominently.
- ✓ Keep displays simple and shoppable (less is often more).
- ✓ Change displays where inventory is broken with something that is in stock.

Merchandise to Match the Customer Journey

- ✓ Entry should be where you inspire. The goal is to wow them quickly.
- ✓ Mid-store is where customers discover. It is where your team can suggest add-ons, build outfits, and show additional categories.
- ✓ Back of store is the destination. Think bestsellers or volume drivers (like milk at the grocery store).
- ✓ Checkout is where the small impulse items or essentials reside.

Maintain Standards Daily

- ✓ Conduct daily visual walk-throughs before the store opens (with specific zones to check).
- ✓ Replenish products before and after peak hours.
- ✓ Assign visual ownership to a specific team member per zone.
- ✓ Rotate product or focal points weekly to keep it feeling fresh.
- ✓ Check the front windows for cleanliness, pristine imagery, or products.

FINAL THOUGHT

Merchandising isn't just about making things look good—it's about making things *move.* Every display, focal point, and product placement should serve a purpose: to inspire, inform, and convert. When your store layout aligns with how customers shop, and your team consistently executes with intention, you transform passive browsing into active buying. Great merchandising doesn't happen once—it happens every day.

Notes

TIME TO TAKE ACTION

- ☐ Take fifteen minutes today to walk your store *like a first-time customer*. Ask: "Is it clear what I should buy? Does it feel fresh and inspiring? Is it easy to shop?"
- ☐ Make one quick improvement that creates immediate visual impact.

DAY 24

Maintain a Clean and Organized Store

SMALL DETAILS, BIG IMPRESSIONS

Cleanliness and organization are silent signals to your customer and your team. A tidy, well-run store says ***we care, we're prepared, and you can trust us***. High-impact store leaders know that mess equals stress, and chaos behind the scenes always makes its way to the floor.

From the front entrance to the back-room shelves, every square foot should feel intentional and cared for. Little things like dust bunnies in the window and burned-out light bulbs have a larger impact than you realize.

Lesson from the Field

I once visited a store where the windows were streaked, the shelves were dusty, and boxes cluttered the fitting rooms. I didn't stay long—and neither did the other shoppers. That experience stuck with me as a reminder: If a store looks neglected, customers feel neglected too. The sad part of this story is that I never shopped that brand again. One bad experience ruined it for me, and for them. What story does your store tell?

> ***"Customers don't see your to-do list. They see your store."***
>
> **—RACHEL WILLIAMSON**

What Great Leaders Do

A clean, organized store is more than just a visual win—it's a reflection of your team's pride, your leadership standards, and your brand's credibility. When every zone—from the shop floor to the back room—runs with intention, customers feel it, and team members rise to meet it. If your apartment is messy, that might be your "acceptable" standard. But your store isn't your apartment. To maximize revenue, your standards must be sky high.

Make a Strong First and Last Impression

- ✓ **General Areas:** Sweep daily, clean doors and glass, and remove clutter—these are your customers' first visual cues.
- ✓ **Floors and Fixtures:** Dust and wipe down shelving, display

risers, and mannequins before opening. Conduct floor checks during slow hours between customers.

- ✓ **Fitting Rooms:** Keep "go-backs" put away, hangers organized, mirrors spotless, and lighting checked daily.
- ✓ **Restrooms:** Clean at open, midday, and close—even if customers rarely use them. Don't forget employee restrooms; your team deserves that same care.
- ✓ **Floor Recovery:** Make it part of hourly routines—don't save it just for closing time.
- ✓ Assign each team member a zone at the start of their shift with a specific visual and cleanliness task. Rotate zones weekly to keep things fresh.

Control the Cash Wrap Chaos

- ✓ The cash wrap should be a clutter-free zone. Stand where the customer stands and see what they see. Minimize personal items, sticky notes, or unrelated paperwork on the counter.
- ✓ Make sure pens, tape, and point of sale (POS) tools are stocked and in a logical location.
- ✓ Keep the back counter clean. Hidden mess impacts energy.
- ✓ Create a three-minute cash wrap reset checklist and post it inside the cabinet or under the drawer.

Set the Standard for Back-Room Discipline

- ✓ New receipts get prioritized and processed—no "graveyard" piles. Work to get goods out to the floor within twenty-four hours of receipt, especially if the sales floor is low on product or specific sizes.
- ✓ Label everything, including back stock, returns to vendors (damages), visuals, markdowns—every box or bin has a home and a label.

- ✓ Set the rule: *If you touch it, you place it properly.* No more stashing in corners.
- ✓ The leader walks the back room once a week with a checklist. Use photos for before/after standards.
- ✓ Ensure safety first with clear aisles, nothing stacked too high, and ladders stored safely.
- ✓ Bulletin boards are updated, old documents discarded, and a personal love—a push pin in the corner of every document 😀.

FINAL THOUGHT

Set the tone, inspect what you expect, and make operational excellence part of your store's DNA. The details *are* the experience.

Notes

TIME TO TAKE ACTION

- ☐ Walk your store before opening and ask: "If this were my first time here, would I be impressed or distracted?"
- ☐ Fix the first thing that feels out of place. Include your team, asking what they see.
- ☐ Then, empower your team to spot and solve clutter all day, every day.

DAY 25

Control Inventory like a Pro

COMMAND YOUR STOCK, CONQUER YOUR SALES

Inventory is money (yours or your employer's) tied up in product form. Whether you're running your own boutique or managing a store for a major brand, controlling inventory is one of the most important ways to drive profitability and prevent lost sales. It's not just about counts and paperwork; it's about ensuring the right product is on the sales floor, in the right size, at the right time. From back-room flow to replenishment routines to markdown accuracy, mastering inventory is a sign of operational excellence.

Lesson from the Field

I was leading one thousand stores for Justice, and we were looking at inventory levels by location with our replenishment partners. On paper, the assortments looked perfect until district leaders told us what would sell. We tested their ideas in one hundred stores, and sales skyrocketed. The lesson was clear: Trust the teams closest to the customer—they know what they need. Adjusting inventory was a key to unlocking revenue potential. Don't wait to be asked; talk to your boss about the inventory you need (or don't need).

"Those closest to the customer have the answers to the business; they just need to be asked."

—RACHEL WILLIAMSON

What Great Leaders Do

Controlling inventory like a pro means being proactive, disciplined, and consistent. Here are three areas that high-impact leaders focus on to keep inventory under control and selling:

Full Floor and Size Runs Intact

A missing size can cost you the sale. Make sure the product your customer wants is where it should be: available and shoppable on the sales floor.

- ✓ Keep items in size order. This helps customers find what they need, and team members can see what needs to be replenished.

Use replenishment reports or a size audit to catch gaps before customers do.

- ✓ Refill empty hooks or shelves before the store opens and again after peak times.
- ✓ On high-volume days, assign one team member to keep the floor full throughout the day.
- ✓ Broken size runs on key items is a red flag. Fill them or remerchandise to avoid missed sales.

Fast and Frequent Product Flow

The back room isn't storage—it's a temporary holding zone. Inventory should flow quickly and frequently to the floor.

- ✓ Create a daily routine for pulling replenishment—ideally before opening and at closing.
- ✓ Minimize midday stockroom traffic; peak hours are for selling, not searching.
- ✓ Avoid the "black hole" effect: If it's living in the back room for days, it's not helping your business.
- ✓ Train your team to see themselves as product movers, not just sellers.
- ✓ Train the replenishment team to use the three-foot rule when stocking the floor—any customers within three feet of them should be acknowledged.

Front and Back Markdown Completion

Markdowns aren't just stickers—they're strategy. Done well, they protect margin and drive sell-through.

- ✓ Ensure all marked-down items on the floor are clearly signed, sized, and easy to find.

✓ Back stock should be marked down *at the same time* as the sales floor product. This ensures as product flows from the back room to the sales floor, the prices are accurate, which prevents confusion for the customer.
✓ Use downtime to audit the clearance area, keeping it organized and compelling.
✓ Track what's moving and what's stuck so you can react quickly.

FINAL THOUGHT

Whether you're a store owner managing every SKU or a manager executing corporate plans, controlling inventory is about precision, urgency, and accountability. When the product flows, sales follow.

Notes

TIME TO TAKE ACTION

- ☐ Today, run a "Zero Empty Spaces" challenge.
- ☐ Before your store opens, walk the floor and hunt down every empty hook, broken size run, or sad-looking fixture. Pull from the back room, rework the display, and make every feature look fully shoppable.
- ☐ Snap before and after pics to train your leaders to see what you see. The goal is to have no empty spaces before the first customer walks in—and keep it that way all day.

DAY 26

Urgency Fuels Operational Excellence

No Lapses, No Excuses

In retail, standards slip the moment urgency fades. Great leaders don't wait for a problem to show up—they anticipate it, audit consistently, and act fast to keep the store running at its best.

Urgency isn't chaos—it's disciplined action. It's walking the floor daily with a critical eye, fixing what's off in the moment, and never letting small lapses snowball into big issues.

A store that runs to standard every day doesn't happen by accident—it happens because the leader refuses to let anything slide.

Lesson from the Field

When I was a district manager for BBW, overseeing the corporate market meant high standards were part of everyday life. Leaders took pride in owning those expectations, and the energy was electric—especially during new product launches. One Saturday at noon, during a busy launch, I walked into a store bursting with customers. The store was packed, the front tables looked chaotic and nearly empty, and two boxes of bestsellers were still unopened in the back room. When I asked about it, the manager said, "We were going to get to it after lunch." In that moment, I understood how overwhelming it was on the floor. But I also saw the opportunity: Every minute those products weren't out was a missed chance to connect with customers and make their day. It wasn't about blame; it was about realizing how urgency fuels great customer experiences and drives results.

That's the danger of losing urgency. Every minute that product sat in the back, we were losing sales. I rolled up my sleeves, pulled the team together, and in twenty minutes those items were stocked and selling. By 4:00 p.m., the store had their sales plan in.

Flawless execution isn't about doing things eventually—it's about doing the *right things* right now. Urgency turns potential into performance.

"Urgency is the heartbeat of high-performing stores— when the team moves with purpose, the results follow."

—RACHEL WILLIAMSON

What Great Leaders Do

Creating a sense of urgency doesn't mean running around or rushing tasks—it means leading a team that is energized, focused, and always moving toward results. High-impact store leaders set the pace, use time wisely, and make every shift feel purposeful.

Set the Pace Daily

Start each day with clear priorities, time-bound goals, and a tone that says, "We're here to win today."

- ✓ Lead a morning huddle that includes sales goals, hot products, and tasks.
- ✓ Assign time frames for key deliverables—e.g., "Let's complete the new floor set by 2:00 p.m."
- ✓ Use countdowns during the day to drive momentum: "One hour left to hit our goal!"
- ✓ Keep energy high by celebrating wins and course-correcting quickly when things stall.

Eliminate the Lull

Complacency kills momentum. Look for—and eliminate—those quiet "dead zone" moments on the floor.

- ✓ Ensure each team member has a clear plan of action between customer interactions.
- ✓ Build a "next task" culture: when the floor is quiet, they know what to tackle.
- ✓ Rotate sales focus every couple of hours to keep the team mentally engaged.
- ✓ Use music, leadership presence, and shout-outs to keep the vibe upbeat and on mission.

Model It Yourself

Leaders set the tone. If you're moving with intention, your team will follow.

- ✓ Be visible and active on the floor—walk with purpose, not just presence.
- ✓ Follow up fast: When a request is made, act or delegate quickly.
- ✓ Avoid "hanging out" in the office during peak times—lead from the front.
- ✓ Use urgent, positive language: "Let's get after it," "This can't wait," "Now's the moment."

FINAL THOUGHT

Urgency is the difference between a store that runs the business versus a business that runs the store. The best leaders set the tone that standards aren't seasonal, weekly, or even daily—they're minute by minute. When urgency is embedded in your store culture, the team moves faster, sells more, and stays more engaged. Customers feel the energy—and that's what keeps them coming back.

Notes

TIME TO TAKE ACTION

- ☐ Today, grab your standards checklist or store audit (or make one) and complete a full-floor review. Fix every lapse immediately and document what you find.
- ☐ If the schedule allows, pair up with one of your leaders and learn what they see!
- ☐ Share wins and gaps with the rest of your team so everyone knows the bar—and that it's not moving.

DAY 27

Master the Final Impression

LEAVE CUSTOMERS WANTING MORE

The checkout is more than just a transaction—it's the final handshake with your customer, the last chance to turn satisfaction into loyalty. To give customers something to talk about with their friends. Yet, it's often overlooked or rushed, turning what should be a moment of celebration into frustration. Long waits, cluttered counters, or unclear pathways can undo the positive experience built throughout the store.

As a high-impact retail leader, you understand that every element here matters—well-trained cashiers, efficient POS systems, and staff readiness to open more registers when two or more customers are in line ensures customers leave feeling valued and eager to return. This is your moment to shine, to reinforce your brand promise, and to lock in the loyalty you've earned.

Lesson from the Field

Early in my retail journey, I was managing a busy flagship store in an upscale, three-level mall. It was a Saturday afternoon, and I was the closing manager. As I was walking in for my shift, I saw that the sales floor was buzzing, customers were being engaged, and the energy was high, until I reached the cash wrap area. There, a long, winding line stretched out, the counter was cluttered with go-backs, and the cashier looked overwhelmed trying to keep up. Customers' irritation was visible; some set their items down and started to walk away. Without hesitation, I dropped my bag, opened a register, and jumped in to help move the line—and salvage as many experiences as I could. Afterward, I pulled the floor supervisor aside—not to assign blame, but to highlight how this one bottleneck could undo hours of great work. Together, we tackled the issue head-on. It was a wake-up call that pushed us to level up our game. The following weekend, the line flowed smoothly, the counters stayed clear, and smiles returned.

That day taught me that the final impression isn't just about speed; it's about respect, clarity, and intention. Nail this moment, and you don't just close a sale—you secure the customer's next visit.

"Your checkout experience is the last word in the conversation. Make it count."

—RACHEL WILLIAMSON

What Great Leaders Do

Optimizing checkout and customer flow isn't just about where the registers are—it's about guiding your customers from the moment they enter to the moment they leave, with as little friction as possible.

Evaluate Customer Flow

- ✓ Are aisles wide enough for strollers, carts, or two people walking side by side?
- ✓ Are high-traffic areas—like fitting rooms, hot product zones, and the checkout—free of visual and physical clutter? Your layout should direct customers naturally toward key merchandise and eventually toward checkout without confusion or obstruction.

Assess the Checkout Experience

- ✓ A poorly managed checkout area can create a frustrating final impression, turning a great visit into a forgettable one.
- ✓ It isn't just about speed; it's about preventing customers from abandoning their purchase at the last hurdle. This means ensuring registers are adequately staffed, systems are running smoothly, and team members are efficient without being rushed. A quick, friendly close reinforces the positive shopping experience and sends the customer out the door feeling great about their purchase—and your brand.
- ✓ If you have mobile POS technology, deploy it to the line during peak times to ring customers out quickly and relieve congestion.
- ✓ POS stations should be clutter-free, fully stocked (bags, receipt tape, gift cards), and working properly. One of my favorite best practices is to change all the register tape at the start of a busy day to make sure it doesn't run out mid-transaction.

- ✓ Impulse displays near checkout should be simple and shoppable, not overwhelming or messy.
- ✓ Team members at checkout should feel confident using the system, offering upsells when appropriate, and closing the interaction on a high note.

Manage Peak Hours

- ✓ Don't let a line undo all your team's great work. The rule is simple: When two to three customers are waiting, open another register.
- ✓ Use traffic data and transaction timing to predict and prevent customer frustration ensuring there are enough cashiers scheduled for peak hours.

FINAL THOUGHT

Walk your store like a customer—from the front door to checkout—and look for bottlenecks. Better yet, ask a friend unfamiliar with the layout to do it. Anywhere they hesitate or feel unsure is a place to improve flow. When customer flow is intuitive and checkout is smooth, shoppers don't just leave with their purchase—they leave with a positive feeling that brings them back.

Notes

TIME TO TAKE ACTION

- ☐ Walk your store with fresh eyes—preferably during peak hours. Observe customer behavior: Where do they pause? Where do they get stuck? Then simplify.
- ☐ Remove physical bottlenecks, keep impulse zones tidy and shoppable, and ensure cash wrap areas are well stocked and staffed.
- ☐ Train team members to make checkouts fast, friendly, and friction-free.

DAY 28

Reduce Shrink

TURN LOSS PREVENTION INTO DAILY LEADERSHIP

Shrink is one of the most overlooked drains on profitability in retail. Whether it's caused by paperwork errors, internal theft, or external theft, loss prevention should be a daily focus.

High-impact leaders build a culture of ownership, awareness, and consistent systems to proactively reduce loss before it happens.

Even honest people can make poor choices when opportunity presents itself. That's why running a tight ship—enforcing bag checks, reviewing paperwork, auditing cash refunds, and keeping the back room clean and organized—isn't just important, it's critical.

Lesson from the Field

Early in my career at the Gap, one of my most trusted employees, someone who came in early, stayed late, and delivered amazing customer experiences, was caught stealing. A surprise inventory count revealed a back-room stash and significant product loss. Letting him go broke my heart, and for a while, I stopped building close relationships with my team out of fear I'd be taken advantage of again. But over time, I realized that guarding myself didn't make me a better leader; leaning into relationships with the right structure and boundaries did.

What Great Leaders Do

Minimize Paperwork Errors

Preventable mistakes—like miscounted shipments, incorrect markdowns, or inaccurate transfers—create gaps in inventory and trust.

High-impact leaders implement clear checks and balances for receiving, inventory counts, and pricing; audit regularly; and use exceptions as teachable moments and foster a culture where accuracy is just as important as speed.

Prevent Internal Theft

When team members see a lack of accountability, they can misuse their POS access by ringing false returns, hiding merchandise, and taking it out with them or giving it to a friend to take out without paying for it. You can avoid potential internal theft opportunities when you:

- ✓ Check transactions weekly, looking for potential fraud with returns and voids.
- ✓ Rotate responsibilities and avoid patterns that allow unchecked behavior.
- ✓ Reinforce expectations and consequences during onboarding and ongoing training.
- ✓ Check for stashed products (a disorganized back room creates opportunity).
- ✓ Enforce policies like bag checks, use of lockers, etc.

Deter External Theft

Loss from outside the organization—whether through theft or return fraud—demands proactive, intentional management. High-impact leaders:

- ✓ Design store layouts, signage, and team presence to create a visible, unwelcoming environment for theft.
- ✓ Train every team member to consistently engage customers, spot suspicious behavior, and enforce policies—firmly but fairly. Remember, the goal is deterrence, not confrontation.
- ✓ Collaborate closely with loss prevention experts to analyze data, identify patterns, and deploy targeted solutions that protect both people and profit.

Great leaders treat loss prevention as a strategic priority—it's about safeguarding the business without compromising the customer experience.

FINAL THOUGHT

Loss prevention isn't just about catching theft—it's about leading with intention, creating structure, and building a culture where everyone feels responsible for protecting the business. When you make shrink reduction part of the daily rhythm—not a once-a-year event—you strengthen trust, improve accuracy, and ultimately protect your team's ability to grow and thrive.

Notes

TIME TO TAKE ACTION

Integrate shrink prevention into your daily operations. Use team huddles to keep it top of mind, reinforce the why behind each policy, and empower team members to take action when something doesn't look right.

- ☐ Choose one shrink category and spotlight it in your daily huddle.
- ☐ Make it visual and practical.
- ☐ Demonstrate the mistake or risk.
- ☐ Coach the team on the right behaviors to prevent it.

Power in the Pause

WEEK 4 RECAP: RUN A TIGHTER OPERATION, DRIVE BIGGER RESULTS

This week was about where solid leadership meets smart execution. This section is all about how great leaders make the store *run like a machine* without losing the human touch; the *engine* of your store is scheduling, inventory, merchandising, and in-store execution. You moved from leadership in theory to operational mastery in practice.

Week 4 Focus Areas

Day 22—Scheduling for Productivity

A great schedule supports the customer, the business, and the team. Schedule to match traffic—not tenure—and protect peak hours. Right people, right place, right time.

Day 23—Merchandising for Sales Impact

Great merchandising tells a story, drives traffic flow, and makes buying easy. Make every table, rack, and display work hard for you.

Day 24—Maintain a Clean and Organized Store

Clean stores sell more. Customers and team members notice what you tolerate. A tidy store, cash wrap, and back room reflect your leadership.

Day 25—Control Inventory like a Pro

It's not just about counts and paperwork; it's about ensuring the right product is on the sales floor, in the right size, at the right time. From back-room flow to replenishment routines to markdown accuracy, mastering inventory is a sign of operational excellence.

Day 26—Urgency Fuels Operational Excellence

Urgency isn't chaos—it's clarity, focus, and energy. Great leaders pace the day and keep teams moving with purpose and executing to your standards.

Day 27—Master the Final Impression

The last impression matters. The cash wrap is your place to eliminate friction, reduce wait times, and create a checkout experience that ends on a high note.

Day 28—Reduce Shrink and Build Awareness

Loss prevention is everyone's job. Train your team to stay alert, protect the product, and act with confidence, not fear.

REFLECT AND RESET

Which operational habit had the biggest impact this week?

____

____

____

What part of your store needs a fresh set of eyes—or a higher standard?

____

____

____

Where can you tighten systems without losing heart?

____

____

____

RACHEL-*ism*

Operational excellence doesn't just protect your business—it elevates your leadership. The details always matter. It is often said, "We don't rise to the level of our goals, we fall to the level of our standards."

WEEK 5

Grow the Leader Within

REAL WINS, REAL LESSONS

When I stepped into my new district leadership role, the stores I inherited were struggling, sales were slipping, teams were disconnected, and consistency was missing. I knew that showing up with checklists wouldn't fix what was broken. Instead, I decided to start with something deeper: listening.

I visited every store, walking the sales floor and back rooms, asking the leaders simple but powerful questions: *What do you see? What do you feel? What do you wish could change?* Their answers revealed more than numbers ever could.

Then I called everyone together for a breakfast meeting. I placed an empty chair in the center of the room. As they filed into the room, a few curious eyes glanced at it. "Who's going to sit there?" someone asked.

I tapped the chair gently and said, "This seat belongs to our most important guest—the customer. Every choice we make, every word we speak, should honor the person who would be sitting right here."

The room fell silent. At first, it felt strange—a little awkward. But that empty chair stayed. Month after month at every breakfast meeting, it was there, reminding us of who truly mattered.

And with it, a shift began.

Each meeting, I'd ask: "If a customer could hear our conversations when they were not around, would they feel loved? If they got a demo at the sink, would they feel cared for? If they sat in this room, would they know they're valued?"

Slowly, the chair became more than just a prop. It became a way of thinking, a new habit. Teams started holding themselves accountable—not because I told them to, but because they imagined that customer watching. Tones softened. Floors were tidied without prompting. Urgency took on new meaning.

One day, a store manager taped a smiling customer's photo to the back of the chair. "Now she's always watching," she said with a grin.

Months later, when our regional leader came for a visit, sales were climbing, and the energy was different. Curious, she asked, "What changed? How did this team find such alignment?"

I smiled and told her the story of the chair. It wasn't just about improving the stores—it was about discovering the leader within each person, about seeing beyond titles and tasks to the heart of leadership itself.

True leadership doesn't come from a title or a role. It comes from the courage to look inward, to lead with empathy, and to put those you serve at the center—even when no one else is watching.

That chair? It was never empty. It held the voice that matters most: the customer's—and each leader's call to purpose.

DAY 29

Grow Yourself with Intention

LEADERSHIP STARTS WITH HOW YOU LEAD YOURSELF

Leadership is a journey, not a destination. To grow with intention means committing to mindset shifts, building new habits, and sharpening skills—whether that's tuning into leadership podcasts during your commute, diving into books that challenge your thinking, seeking honest feedback (even when it stings), or learning from the people around you. Being a student of both how to grow your business and yourself should be a nonnegotiable.

In retail, where the pace never slows and pressure is high, your growth mindset keeps you sharp, adaptable, and ready for whatever's next. Great leaders aren't born—they're built. And that building starts with you.

Lesson from the Field

My successful career has been defined by one constant: my unwavering commitment to growing myself. Two examples follow.

- Choose one word for the year. This simple yet powerful practice provides a clear compass to guide your decisions, focus, and growth. Your chosen word becomes a North Star, helping you prioritize what matters most, align with your values, and build intentional habits. Rather than juggling many goals, you anchor your mindset and actions around one meaningful theme, making it easier to stay motivated, make aligned choices, and track progress. Jon Gordon's *One Word* is a fantastic, quick read to get started.
- Pick a leadership book to read each quarter. I've built a large library over the years, and a great way to start is by focusing on what you want to grow. One of my favorites is *The Power of Positive Leadership* by Jon Gordon—it fills leadership gaps and fuels motivation. Some books have been better than others, but what matters most is the habit of continuous learning.

Keep learning. Keep growing. Your leadership depends on it.

What Great Leaders Do

Lead With Curiosity and Humility

- ✓ Actively invest in becoming better every day.
- ✓ Ask for feedback and apply it without defensiveness, embracing it as a gift for growth.
- ✓ Dedicate time regularly to reading, listening to podcasts, or learning from mentors who challenge your thinking and sharpen your mindset.
- ✓ Stay curious: about the business, your impact, and how to improve.
- ✓ Approach challenges as opportunities to learn rather than problems to avoid.

Cultivate Self-Awareness and Emotional Intelligence

- ✓ Reflect honestly on your strengths and areas to improve, owning your impact on others.
- ✓ Pause to understand your emotions before responding, maintaining composure in stressful situations.
- ✓ Recognize and respect diverse perspectives, fostering an inclusive environment where all voices matter.

Take Consistent Action to Build Your Leadership Skills

- ✓ Set personal development goals and track your progress with discipline.
- ✓ Step outside your comfort zone regularly to practice new skills or lead in unfamiliar situations.
- ✓ Model the behaviors and attitudes you want to see, inspiring others through your example.

Manage Your Energy

Strong leaders know that how they show up affects everyone around them—especially in fast-paced retail environments.

- ✓ Regulate your mindset before every shift—choosing positivity and presence.
- ✓ Recognize burnout signs early and take steps to reset.
- ✓ Walk in with energy that lifts the team, not drains it.

FINAL THOUGHT

When you grow yourself, you rise—and bring everyone with you.

Notes

TIME TO TAKE ACTION

- ☐ Pick one area of leadership you want to grow: communication, decision-making, conflict resolution, or emotional control.
- ☐ For the next seven days, practice improving that skill in your daily work. Growth isn't a title change—it's a mindset shift.

DAY 30

Leave a Lasting Impact

GREAT LEADERS DON'T JUST RUN STRONG STORES, THEY LEAVE A LASTING IMPACT

Your influence goes far beyond today's sales or this week's floor set. The way you lead shapes your team's culture, builds customer loyalty, and develops future leaders. True leadership is about more than being in charge—it's about making a difference that lasts.

We often think about legacy only as we get older, but it's something we should consider at every stage of our careers. When you lead with your legacy in mind, it guides your decisions, inspires others, and creates a ripple effect that carries forward long after your shift ends.

Lesson from the Field

I still remember a team member from years ago who reached out to tell me that something I said in a one-on-one changed how she viewed herself as a leader and gave her the courage to go after a promotion. I barely remembered the conversation, but she never forgot it.

That's the thing about leadership: Your words and actions echo far beyond the moment. Make them count.

What Great Leaders Do

Mentor the Next Generation

- ✓ Invest time in growing your team, not just in skills, but in confidence and mindset. When taking on new teams, I love using *StrengthsFinder 2.0* by Tom Rath to unlock unique talents and boost collaboration.
- ✓ Share what you've learned, coach them through challenges, and speak potential into their future.
- ✓ Your leadership legacy isn't what you accomplish—it's what you empower others to do after you.

Lead with Consistency and Integrity

Show up with the same energy and standards every day. By being consistent in your values, work ethic, and follow-through, you build a culture of stability and high standards.

Elevate the Brand Experience

- ✓ Don't just run a store—represent the brand. Be the example of what it looks like when vision, values, and execution come together.
- ✓ Create an experience guests and team members remember—for all the right reasons.

Be the Store Everyone Wants to Work In

Your goal? A team that's proud to wear the badge, that grows together, and that attracts great talent. Culture is contagious. Make yours one that inspires excellence, joy, and personal growth.

Think Beyond the Metrics

Yes, sales matter. But impact includes how you show up during tough times, how you lead during change, and how you leave people feeling every day. Your influence isn't measured only in dollars—it's measured in people.

FINAL THOUGHT

Behaviors are more caught than taught. When you model these behaviors consistently, your team will naturally adopt them. True leadership is measured by the legacy you leave in the lives you've lifted.

TIME TO TAKE ACTION

- ☐ Identify one team member this week whose growth you've influenced—then take five minutes to tell them the difference they've made and how you see their future potential. Small moments create a lasting impact.

Power in the Pause

WEEK 5 RECAP: LEAD WITH PURPOSE, FINISH STRONG

This final week was about leadership that lasts—holding the line, building a legacy, and preparing for what's next. The habits you've built over the last thirty days aren't just practices—they're *proof* that you're leading on purpose.

Week 5 Focus Areas

Day 29—Grow Yourself with Intention

Great leaders are not born; they are built, and that starts with growing yourself.

Day 30—Leave a Lasting Impact

Your leadership lives on in how your team leads when you're not there. Mentor others, live your values, and create ripple effects that last beyond today.

Growth doesn't stop here. Reflect on your wins, identify your next challenge, and keep leading with clarity and consistency. The best leaders are always learning.

REFLECT AND RESET

What are you most proud of from these thirty days?

What habit or behavior do you want to double down on going forward?

How will you keep growing as a leader?

RACHEL-*ism*

The goal was never to check a box—it was to raise your standard. You did that. Now, keep going.

Conclusion

From Learning to Long-Term Transformation

Congratulations. You've just completed thirty days of purposeful growth as a store leader—and that's no small accomplishment. You've challenged old habits, adopted new mindsets, and leaned into practical strategies that can transform your store, your team, and yourself. But this is not the end. It's the beginning of what's possible.

REFLECT ON YOUR GROWTH

Before you rush back into your daily whirlwind, take a moment to pause and reflect:

- ✓ What behaviors have shifted in you as a leader?
- ✓ Which topics hit home the most?
- ✓ What feedback have you received from your team?
- ✓ How has your store responded to the changes?

Flip back through your notes or dog-eared pages. Circle the three to five areas that had the biggest impact. These are your leadership anchors—return to them often.

SET MEANINGFUL GOALS

Now that you've seen what's possible, set one to two specific leadership goals. Make them measurable. Give them a timeline. And tie them back to outcomes that matter. Here are some thought starters:

- ✓ Grow your store's conversion results.
- ✓ Improve your team's selling behaviors.
- ✓ Reduce shrink through operational ownership.
- ✓ Coach an associate into a leadership role.

Write them down. Share them with someone who can support you. Make progress, not excuses.

KEEP THE MOMENTUM GOING

Leadership isn't a one-time push—it's a consistent practice. To stay sharp, try this:

- ✓ Schedule a monthly leadership self-check.
- ✓ Pick one section from this book to focus on each quarter.
- ✓ Stay connected to other leaders who challenge and inspire you.

Would your management team benefit from this book? Give them your copy or buy them their own. You aren't going to run the store 24/7. Teaching your team to run a great store is key to maximizing your store's revenue!

Need help keeping the momentum? I'd love to walk alongside you.

- ✓ Subscribe to my Substack newsletter at https://runninggreatstores.substack.com/
- ✓ Book a workshop or coaching session for your team
- ✓ Or simply reach out at Rachel@runninggreatstores.com

FINAL THOUGHT

Leadership isn't about having all the answers. It's about staying curious, showing up with consistency, and creating an environment where people and performance thrive. You've got this. Now, go lead well. Leave your mark. And run a great store.

xoxo,

Rachel

About the Author

My journey into apparel brick-and-mortar retail began at sixteen, a wide-eyed store associate quickly promoted to store manager of a locally owned preppy boutique—and that initial spark has since ignited a lifelong passion.

For decades, I've been driven by a singular purpose: to craft exceptional customer experiences and drive sales growth through robust store leadership and operational excellence. This dedication quickly earned me a reputation as a collaborative high performer, consistently sought out to revitalize underperforming stores, districts, regions, projects, and teams. My ability to solve complex problems and deliver tangible results led to consistent promotions throughout my career with multibillion-dollar companies.

Now, as the founder of Running Great Stores Retail Consulting & Leadership Training, I partner with retail brands to achieve operational excellence in their physical locations. My mission is straightforward: to guide retailers in building stores that not only operate at the highest level but also consistently deliver on their unique brand promise—ultimately leading to increased revenue.

Over the years, I've helped direct-to-consumer brands successfully transition into brick-and-mortar spaces, scaled national rollouts, built retail playbooks from the ground up, and trained hundreds of store managers and field leaders to become confident, results-driven retail professionals.

I'm certified in the Energy Bus, the Power of Positive Leadership, and the Power of a Positive Team and regularly lead keynotes and workshops that shift culture and drive performance. My approach blends strategy with real-world experience, offering practical tools and repeatable processes that leaders can apply immediately.

Above all, I believe great stores are built from the inside out—through strong leadership, consistent execution, and teams who know exactly how to win.

www.ingramcontent.com/pod-product-compliance
Lightning Source LLC
Chambersburg PA
CBHW071559210326
41597CB00019B/3314

* 9 7 8 1 5 4 4 5 5 0 9 8 5 *